TOSCANINI

Book Design by Albert Karsten

Copyright© 1987 Treves Publishing Company, a Division of
Elite Publishing Corporation.
120 East 56th Street
New York, New York 10022

Library of Congress Catalog Card Number: 86-24923
ISBN 0-918367-16-6

Portraits of Greatness: Trade Mark Reg. No. 1,368,932

These pages: Arturo Toscanini, bronze by Dario Viterbo, donated by Victor Civita to the City of Rio de Janeiro on the occasion of the centennial of the birth of Toscanini, 1967; Teatro
Municipal, Rio de Janeiro, Brazil.

Cover: *Toscanini, portrait by Arturo Rietti (1863-1943)*;
Milan, Museo Teatrale alla Scala

Portraits of Greatness®
Published series of pictorial biographies
Series I Verdi
        Mozart
        Beethoven
        Chopin
        Dante
(First published in Italian under the title "I Grandi di Tutti i
Tempi", copyright 1965, Arnoldo Mondadori Editore, SpA,
Milan.)

Series II Puccini
        Rossini
        Respighi
        Giordano
        Gershwin
        Toscanini
(By Treves Publishing Company, a division of Elite Publishing
Company. Each volume and title series copyrighted.)

Endpapers: front, Toscanini rehearsing at Teatro Vittorio
Emanuele, Turin, 1898; back, Toscanini conducting NBC Symphony, photo by Robert Hupka.

Graphic Coordinator, Sabino Lenoci, Milano, Italy.

Printed in Italy, october 1987 — Grafiche Lithos,
Carugate (Milano).

Printed on Cartiera Burgo paper R-400/130 grams.

PORTRAITS OF GREATNESS

TOSCANINI

by John W. Freeman and Walfredo Toscanini

**TREVES
PUBLISHING
COMPANY**

Arturo Toscanini was born in a working-class section of Parma called Oltretorrente, "across the river." At left, seen before its modern restoration as a museum, the modest house at No. 13 Borgo San Giacomo (today Borgo Tanzi), where his parents practiced the tailoring trade. It was there, in the room shown at bottom, that he was born.

Parma, a former duchy, is one of the principal cities of northern central Italy. Its octagonal Baptistry (right) is considered one of the country's architectural glories. It was to this imposing structure that Claudio Toscanini had to bring his newborn and only son, at the insistence of his propriety-minded wife, to have the child registered and baptized.

I. MODEST BEGINNINGS

March 26, 1867. The early spring sun was still climbing when Claudio Toscanini, a tailor from the Oltretorrente (Across the River), made his way unnoticed across the Ponte di Mezzo and down the Via della Repubblica, the main thoroughfare of Parma. In his arms was not tailoring to be delivered to a customer but a baby, born the day before, to be registered at the Baptistry—an octagonal building, one of the architectural glories of Italy. He didn't go willingly. Claudio, a local character, was an ardent patriot for an Italian republic, anticlerical and anti-monarchist. But this easygoing man had a strict wife, the former Paolina Montani. It was important to her to observe the formalities.

Standing by Claudio that day was his friend Francesco Campanini, blacksmith and fellow patriot, who was willing to serve as witness to the birth registration but refused to witness the baptism. Both were fathers of future musicians. Claudio's son, Arturo Alessandro, was to become one of the world's most famous conductors; Francesco's sons Italo and Cleofonte were to make their names as tenor and conductor, respectively.

Parma is a city of unique colors. The terra-cotta, verdant greens, brick reds, deep blues and ochers of its buildings match the temperament of the citizens. They are known as outspoken and independent—especially at the Teatro Regio, the city's opera house. Claudio Toscanini sometimes sang in the chorus there, and when Arturo was four, he was taken to his first opera, Verdi's *Un Ballo in Maschera.* Knowing the melodies from home, he tried to sing along with the performance and even "corrected" one of the soloists, who was doing an aria differently from how he had heard it.

The Toscanini family came from Tuscany—the name means "little Tuscans"—settling to the north. Claudio's father, Angelo, ran a spinning mill in Cortemaggiore, near Roncole, birthplace of Giuseppe Verdi. Independent from the first, Claudio had run away from home after a fight with his father, moving to Parma to find work as a tailor. The Toscaninis, though poor by present-day standards, lived comfortably for those uncertain times. Parma had just become part of the Kingdom of Italy under Victor Emmanuel II.

Seen from the air, Parma's Piazza del Duomo (Cathedral Square) shows the Baptistry next door to the bell-tower of the Cathedral (left). At the center of the city's cultural life stands the Teatro Regio, with its plain façade (middle left) and ornate auditorium (middle right), the royal box located above the main entrance. This theater is known for its exacting audience.

It was here that the four-year-old Arturo Toscanini heard and saw his first opera, Verdi's Un Ballo in Maschera, singing along with the soloists the melodies he had heard at home. Left: street scene. At foot of page, a view across the river—a seasonal "torrent," sometimes little more than a trickle— toward the Oltretorrente district, where his family lived.

The parents of Arturo Toscanini, seen below around the time of their marriage, were a contrasting couple: the excitable but easy-going Claudio, sometime tailor who fought and was imprisoned during the wars for Italian independence, and the stern, realistic Paola (Paolina) Montani, a seamstress, whose hard life left little time for her four children.

The eldest child, Arturo (foot of page), was the only boy and therefore the future breadwinner. The picture shows him at the age of three, after he had survived a sickly infancy but before he showed signs of the musical talent that would determine his future. Claudio, musically inclined himself, was not averse to having a musician in the family.

II. FAMILY BACKGROUND

Arturo Toscanini's character owed something to both parents. From his mother, Paolina (1840-1924), disciplined, uncompromising and severe, the young man absorbed a realistic view of life and an exigent set of standards. His father, Claudio (1833-1906), was entirely different. From this excitable, fun-loving man he learned idealism, sensitivity and a firebrand devotion to Italy's independence from foreign rule. Deserting the king's army to join Garibaldi's rebel troops, Claudio escaped execution as a deserter but eventually was forced to spend three years in prison. After his marriage in 1866, he rejoined the revolutionaries for the Third War of Independence, serving again under Garibaldi in the Trentino to the north. According to family legend, Arturo was conceived one night when his father managed to slip away from a troop train near Parma and come home.

In later life, Arturo Toscanini would recall, "My mother never loved me. My aunt loved me." Once, seeing how his father's irresponsible ways had hurt his mother, the boy spoke out against Claudio—only to be rebuked angrily by his mother, who defended the head of the family. Sewing at home, trying to make ends meet, Paolina had little time for the amenities of family life. It made her job no easier that Arturo seemed sickly—a candidate for tuberculosis, in the doctor's opinion. Languishing on a diet of gruel prescribed for his delicate health, he begged one day for the *pasta e fagioli* he saw the others eating. Taking pity on him, as he presumably didn't have long to live anyway, the family offered him some of this hearty dish. From then on, he recalled, his health improved on a normal diet.

Apart from his mother's sisters and her parents, the boy was cared for by Medea Massari, an apprentice who came to help with the sewing. Arturo fiddled on a stringed instrument the young woman had made for him from a hollowed-out corncob, and she took the five-year-old to her parents' house, where he touched the keys of a real spinet for the first time. At eight, when he entered the local elementary school, one of his teachers noted his seriousness and excellent memory. At her home she taught him the rudiments of music. Eventually she spoke to his parents, suggesting he be sent to music school.

At left, the boy Arturo at nine with his sister Narcisa, who died in childhood, and their Aunt Esterina, one of the mother's sisters, who helped bring him up. Below at left, father Claudio's formal portrait wearing his red Garibaldi shirt—his proudest possession. Bottom left, campaign medals awarded him, showing king and Garibaldi.

A painting by S. De Albertis (below) depicts the historic meeting between Giuseppe Garibaldi and King Vittorio Emanuele II at Teano, where they joined forces to free Italy from foreign rule. Bottom, the Battle of Bezzecca, July 21, 1866, painted by F. Zennaro. There, the year before Arturo's birth, Claudio Toscanini shared the revolutionists' victory.

At the age of nine, Toscanini was admitted to the Regio Scuola di Music (Royal School of Music, today the Arrigo Boito Conservatory) in Parma, and the school became his home the following year, when he earned a boarding scholarship. Despite a sometimes stubborn temperament, he was a diligent, absorbed student, whose life revolved around music.

Housed in a former monastery (below), austere in both outward and inner appearance (bottom, the collective dormitory room), the Conservatory was nevertheless a proud institution that upheld Parma's traditional devotion to culture and the arts, especially music. Discipline and curriculum followed a strict pedagogical pattern.

III. STUDENT YEARS

In many places, the idea of having a family's only son, the eventual breadwinner, become a musician would have been regarded as a calamity. Not in Parma, where the arts had firm roots and musicians were regarded with respect. Claudio Toscanini liked the idea of having a musician in the family. But how could the boy meet the entrance requirements for the Royal School of Music? After taking some piano lessons locally, he was summoned for an interview by the directors of the conservatory. "What's the difference between a tone and a sound?" he was asked. Though not yet sophisticated enough to know the answer—one has pitch, the other doesn't—Arturo showed natural aptitude and was taken as an "external" student, living at home. This meant the family had to scrape together the first year's tuition. His excellent marks, however, assured board and scholarship the second year.

Barring occasional disciplinary problems resulting from his independent spirit, he remained a model student. In fact he became a musical fanatic, sometimes selling his meat rations to fellow students for a little money to buy printed music. Housed in a former Carmelite monastery, the school had monastic accommodations. For nine years it became Toscanini's home. His mother, only a short distance away, never visited him; she said she lacked the proper clothes. After a year devoted to the basics, he was assigned an instrument—the cello—as his major course of study. Once he found himself locked in a practice room, desperately needing to go to the toilet but unable to escape. After due consideration, he decided his only recourse was to use the cello for a receptacle.

As an advanced student, Toscanini became eligible to play in the Teatro Regio orchestra, where he discovered Wagner—"the greatest composer of our time," he declared, despite his reverence for Verdi. He graduated with highest marks in cello and composition, plus a prize as the outstanding student. To earn a living, Toscanini's sights were set on a career as cellist. Meanwhile, he had been composing songs, mostly for singers of his acquaintance. He might have been a composer as well. But he would have been a minor composer—and Toscanini was never one to settle for second best.

Wearing the simple but rather elegant uniform shown at left, students lived and worked under the watchful, paternal eye of Giusto Dacci (lower left), director of the Conservatory. They studied and practiced their instruments in small rooms like the one at center below, taking music from the well-stocked library, below right.

At bottom left, the program for a concert held on May 25, 1884, shortly before Toscanini's graduation, shows him in a triple capacity as composer, conductor (of his own pieces) and cello soloist (in a virtuoso piece by Emile Dunkler, a well-known cellist of the day). The courtyard of the Conservatory as it appears now, bottom right.

PROGRAMMA

PARTE PRIMA

E. Preti (Alunno)

1. *Sinfonia in Re per Orchestra diretta dall' Autore.*

J. Demersseman.

2. *Fantasia per Flauto* (Op. 43.) . . . . { Alfredo Casoli

H. Vieuxtemps.

3. *La Caccia — Capriccio per Violino* . . . { Eurialo Allodi

G. Donizetti.

4. *Aria nell'Opera* **Lucrezia Borgia** (Come è bello) { Enrichetta Guarnieri

E. Dunkler.

5. *Introduzione e Polonese per Violoncello* (Op. 24) { Arturo Toscanini

A. Toscanini. (Alunno)

6. *Andante e Scherzo per Orchestra diretti dall' Autore.*

IV. OUT INTO THE WORLD

Arturo Toscanini continued to compose music until 1891. In 1888, however, he attended the Italian premiere of Wagner's *Tristan und Isolde* at Bologna. The strength and novelty of the work overwhelmed him, and midway in the performance he resolved not to become a composer. His music was well-crafted student work, and in the final years of his life he still remembered it. But it did not meet the stringent standards he set for himself.   Fresh out of the conservatory, Toscanini continued to play cello in the Teatro Regio orchestra, absorbing the repertory and the ways of the opera house at first hand. Then, in the summer of 1885, at age eighteen, he was picked as first cellist (an honor for one so young) for a touring troupe organized by an impresario named Claudio Rossi to perform in South America the following spring. Besides practicing the cello, he coached and accompanied the singers during the sea voyage. On a stopover in Cadiz, Spain, he passed his nineteenth birthday.

In those days, long before the invention of air conditioning, there were no summer seasons in European theaters, and summer festivals—other than Bayreuth, the Wagner shrine—were not yet a major enterprise. To find work during the summer, Italian musicians often signed up for the trip to South America, where the winter season ran through the European summer months. Receptive audiences were guaranteed by the large number of Italians and other Europeans who had made their homes in South American cities. But since there were no union contracts protecting the artists, the trip involved an element of chance. Lacking funds in advance to pay for the whole tour, the organizers had to depend on fees and ticket sales to meet the payroll and cover the fare home.

To make sure of success, Rossi had engaged internationally known singers, including baritone (formerly tenor) Paul Lhérie—who, Toscanini learned after working with him a whole season, had sung the first Don José in Bizet's *Carmen*—soprano Nadia Boulicioff, bass Gaetano Roveri and Russian tenor Nicolai Figner with his wife, Medea Mei-Figner, who in 1890 would take leading roles in the world premiere of Tchaikovsky's *Queen of Spades.* Working with such artists was invaluable experience.

By the time he finished at the Conservatory, Toscanini had composed quite a few songs, some of them published (facing page), as well as orchestra pieces for his thesis. A few years after graduation, his life was dramatically affected by discovering Wagner's Tristan und Isolde at the Teatro Comunale in Bologna, shown at left and below.

Meanwhile, at eighteen, he was made first cellist for an opera company to visit South America in the summer of 1885. This placed him in daily contact with tenor Nicolai Figner (below left, trick double exposure) and his wife (below center), as well as French baritone Paul Lhérie—ten years before, as a tenor, the first Don José in Bizet's Carmen.

Emperor Dom Pedro II of Brazil, below, lent his name to the opera house in Rio de Janeiro (bottom) where Arturo Toscanini made his emergency debut as conductor, saving the touring troupe's Aida. *Top of facing page: Giuseppe Verdi, composer of* Aida, *drawn by Tissot for* Vanity Fair. *Right, announcement of the fateful* Aida *performance in Brazil.*

Foot of facing page: Leopoldo Miguéz (left), Italian-trained Brazilian maestro whose withdrawal threatened Aida *with cancellation; Carlo Superti (center), assistant conductor, prevented by audience from replacing Miguéz; and Eugenia Mantelli (right), mezzo-soprano (later with Metropolitan Opera), with whom Toscanini was tarrying at performance time.*

After two months in São Paulo, where they opened with Donizetti's *La Favorita*, the company moved up the Brazilian coast to Rio de Janeiro. The local conductor, Leopoldo Miguéz, though he had studied in Italy, was judged incompetent by the performers, who wanted him to step down in favor of their Italian assistant conductor, Carlo Superti. In Rio, before the second performance—*Aida* on June 30, 1886—Miguéz quit. The audience, who regarded him as a favorite native son, demonstrated against Superti, who tried to mount the podium.

The night of that performance, Toscanini had lost track of the time. At the musicians' *pensione*, he was going over Schubert songs (and perhaps thinking of dallying) with Eugenia Mantelli, a mezzo-soprano from the company. Suddenly realizing he would be late and might be fined or be unable to collect his pay, the young cellist caught a trolley to the theater. What he found, instead of a performance in progress, was an audience in uproar. The company members were upset: if the performance did not go on, no one would be paid. Toscanini's colleagues knew he had the repertory memorized, and several urged him to conduct. Escaping from pit to stage, he was urged by the chorus, including a woman from his hometown with tears in her eyes. Reluctantly he agreed, but when Rossi offered him his frock coat, Toscanini said he would keep his orchestra uniform.

When the unknown beardless youth seated himself at the conductor's desk, the audience's hostility changed to curiosity, and he was allowed to begin. He gained confidence as he went on, reminding himself not to make a cellist's bowing movements (with arm lowered) but to give visible signals to the stage. By the end of the opera, when the audience gave him an ovation, he realized his copy of the score was still open to page one. Relying entirely on memory, he had made and survived two mistakes, which he remembered for the rest of his life. The local press hailed a remarkable discovery, and Rossi asked him to lead the other eleven operas of the season. For this he received no raise in pay, though he was given proceeds from one performance as a bonus. When Rossi disappeared, owing money, at the end of the season, the musicians had to give a benefit concert to pay their way home.

Role models for nineteen-year-old Toscanini were such noted older maestros as Alessandro Pomè, Franco Faccio and Giuseppe Martucci, left to right below. Pomè led the world premiere of Puccini's Manon Lescaut in 1893, Faccio that of Verdi's Otello in 1887 (with Toscanini in the orchestra), while Martucci, also a composer, favored symphonic repertory.

The first opera that Toscanini conducted in Italy was Catalani's Edmea in Turin, November 4, 1886. In the newspaper cartoon at foot of page he is shown as "Il Bambino Toscanini," a child prodigy, sitting on the score rather than reading it, while Catalani, skinny as a beanpole, stands on-stage acknowledging applause with the singers.

VI. BEGINNINGS OF A CAREER

The late nineteenth century was an era of major conductors in Italy, all artistic descendants of Angelo Mariani (1821-73), the first concertmaster to earn fame with a baton. Alessandro Pomé, Franco Faccio, Luigi Mancinelli, Edoardo Mascheroni, Giuseppe Martucci and Leopoldo Mugnone were all in their late twenties or older when Toscanini, a youth of nineteen, came home from South America. To gain experience and earn a living, he looked for more work as a cellist. But singers who had worked with him in South America had something else in m.nd. Nicolai Figner and his wife brought Toscanini to Milan to coach them in new roles and accompany their auditions at the Teatro alla Scala. Meanwhile, they gave him the score of a new opera, *Edmea* by Alfredo Catalani, to play through, concealing the composer (unknown to Toscanini) in an adjoining room.

Stepping from the shadows after the reading, Catalani found it unbelievable that Toscanini was seeing the score for the first time. Befriending the young man, he asked for him to be appointed conductor of the Turin premiere of *Edmea* on November 4, 1886, his professional conducting debut in Italy. By the end of the year, prospects were good enough for Toscanini to send for his family to join him in Milan, capital of the Italian music world. His father found work with a Milanese tailoring firm. Years after, recalling the tenor Figner, Toscanini would say, "I owe him my career."

In early 1887 the talk of musical Italy was the coming world premiere of *Otello* by Giuseppe Verdi, at seventy-three the dean of Italian opera. To be near Verdi, Toscanini joined the orchestra for the first *Otello* at La Scala. During rehearsals under Maestro Faccio, when four solo cellos were introducing the love duet at the end of Act I, Verdi approached the orchestra and asked Toscanini to play a little louder. The young man said nothing—he had been following the instructions written in his part to play *very* softly—but privately thought Verdi was really criticizing the "star" first cellist, Magrini, for playing too loud. Toscanini's opinion of the prima donna, Romilda Pantaleoni, who he thought sang out of tune, he also kept to himself: the soprano was the *innamorata* of Maestro Faccio.

The world premiere of Verdi's Otello (poster at left) at the Teatro alla Scala in Milan (below) on February 5, 1887, was an event of world importance. The leading roles were taken by Romilda Pantaleoni as Desdemona (lower left), Victor Maurel as Iago (center, with the composer) and tenor Francesco Tamagno (right) in the title role.

Scenic and costume designs (bottom) show that no expense was spared in creating a splendid production. Poet Arrigo Boito, himself a composer of the opera Mefistofele, adapted Shakespeare's tragedy Othello for the elderly Verdi, who attended rehearsals and spoke with cellist Toscanini about playing softly to introduce the love duet.

At twenty (left), Toscanini was on his way toward a major conducting career, working at first in cities outside the major centers. Though musical standards were often sadly provincial, the theaters themselves were usually the pride of the town, such as the Teatro Ponchielli in Cremona (interior at bottom), named after famous native son among composers.

Amilcare Ponchielli (below right), whose name the theater in Cremona bears, wrote one big and lasting success—Gioconda, to a text by Arrigo Boito after Victor Hugo. In his day he was renowned and loved as a teacher, numbering among his pupils Pietro Mascagni and Giacomo Puccini, who had been student roommates in Milan.

"Son uomo di teatro," Arturo Toscanini would say all his life—"I'm a theater man." In the Italy of his youth, to be a conductor meant to be an opera conductor, though some high-minded musicians were trying to popularize symphony concerts. It was a world of theaters—every city or town of any pretensions had one. And operatic novelties, both by established masters and by new composers, were constantly being introduced alongside the familiar favorites. Opera houses were places of creativity and entertainment, frequently of lively controversy.

At twenty, Toscanini entered his apprenticeship as a conductor in provincial theaters. Learning the ways of Italian theater performance, he was confronted with decisions. Which traditions made sense artistically, which were based on unthinking routine? The more he heard of encores, for example, the less he liked them—they disturbed the dramatic flow and turned the opera into a carnival. Once, when he refused an encore in Ponchielli's *Gioconda*, an officer in the audience challenged him to a duel. Italians took their opera to heart.

His first short season as a conductor, from December 1887 to February 1888, showed Toscanini how far from ideal the conditions were in the provinces. October, however, brought his conducting debut in Milan. When he appeared at the Teatro Dal Verme, a theater only three years older than he was, *Il Secolo* took note that the new maestro had a mind of his own, refusing to observe the customary traditions in Verdi's *La Forza del Destino*.

He learned scores quickly and got impressive results under less than the best conditions, so work kept coming. As he moved to the more important cities, Toscanini proved the effectiveness of walking out, or threatening to, if his conditions were not met. In one typical encounter, he obliged the impresario to double the number of choristers; in another, to replace many of the orchestra players. At the Politeama in Genoa the following summer (1889), he first met Giulio Gatti-Casazza, an aspiring young impresario from Ferrara, later his administrative partner for many years. And in Brescia in mid-December, Toscanini for the first time led a work by Giacomo Puccini, the thirty-one-year-old composer of *Le Villi*.

Left, the title page of Puccini's first opera, the brief Le Villi, introduced in 1884 at the Teatro Dal Verme, Milan (below right) and led by Toscanini five years later. Below left, the young team who wrote the work, heavily influenced by German romanticism— poet Ferdinando Fontana, twenty-six-year-old composer Puccini. At lower left, sketch for Le Villi.

Larger cities and theaters had begun to beckon to Toscanini. At the Politeama in Genoa he first made the acquaintance of the aspiring impresario Giulio Gatti-Casazza, with whom he is shown at lower right. Trained in naval engineering, Gatti-Casazza sacrificed it for the theater, starting with the Teatro Municipale in Ferrara, his hometown.

With increasing success in his mid-twenties, Arturo Toscanini, though far from wealthy, at that time was able to help his family. He appears below with his surviving sisters, Zina and Ada, flanking their parents, Paolina and Claudio. All in their Sunday best, they may have posed in Milan or at a family reunion in Parma or Genoa.

A dapper dresser throughout his life, Toscanini favored hats, which enhanced his rather short stature and became a kind of trademark with him. The lower picture, one of a series taken in Parma, shows an uncharacteristically dashing, quasi-Bohemian look that may have been influenced by some of the poses struck by Puccini around that time.

VIII. THE REFORMER

At twenty-three, still not working regularly in one place, obliged to put up with the insufficiencies of this or that theater, Arturo Toscanini was starting to find and assert himself. Though obstinate, he was rather quiet by nature and had to learn to insist. Much as he may have regretted hurting others' feelings in the process, he was physically upset when things didn't go well—a bad performance made him feel almost sick—and when he couldn't get the desired results through explanation and repetition, frustration and rage would take over. Colleagues who understood and shared Toscanini's goals were rewarded with a better performance. Others simply felt he was demanding too much.

In Toscanini's early years, when his character was tempered, drastic reforms were needed. Even a major theater like La Scala in Milan did not have a permanent orchestra; instead, the musicians were hired for each season on an ad hoc basis. Lacking steady employment, musicians suffered loss of income, morale and skill. Toscanini insisted on auditions, even for players who had been in the orchestra before. Though many resented this, the press and public were quick to appreciate the improvement in orchestral quality.

Today—thanks in part to Toscanini's reforms—musicians are better trained and organized, have a broader education and have risen to a position of salaried respectability. They are likely to be proficient, responsible, knowledgeable. The village musician, the town band, have been left behind in an age where records, radio and television accustom a wide audience to high standards. And the "terrible temper" of a Toscanini no longer is needed.

A new decade had begun—it was now 1890—when, after four months of unemployment over the summer, Toscanini was named assistant to Maestro Edoardo Mascheroni for a season of operas in Barcelona, Spain. Mascheroni was aware of the young man's reputation. To put Toscanini to the test, Mascheroni assigned him a particularly difficult opera to prepare, Bellini's *I Capuleti e i Montecchi*. The plan backfired when the opera succeeded with the public, so Mascheroni withdrew it after three performances. Toscanini had become a force in the music world.

Toscanini seldom conducted operas by Sicilian composer Vincenzo Bellini (left), feeling it was too hard to cast them, but he did prepare Bellini's Romeo and Juliet story, I Capuleti e i Montecchi, *while an assistant to* Edoardo Mascheroni (lower left). *It was Mascheroni who led the world premiere of Verdi's last opera,* Falstaff, *in 1893.*

Below, the Teatre del Liceu in Barcelona, where Toscanini worked briefly as Mascheroni's assistant. Like the Teatro Colón in Buenos Aires, this house has a reputation for short, brilliant seasons with distinguished guests. At bottom, the Carlo Felice, one of the leading theaters of Genoa— the other being the Politeama— where Toscanini conducted.

Dominant forces in the world of opera, then as now, were giants Giuseppe Verdi (left) and Richard Wagner, both passionately admired by Toscanini. Their works posed a challenge to young composers, such as the aspiring Pietro Mascagni and Ruggero Leoncavallo, caricatured left and right at bottom, though both had a popular following.

Mascagni and Leoncavallo wrote numerous works but failed to equal their early, enduring success with Cavalleria Rusticana *and* Pagliacci, *respectively, which eventually became permanent double-bill mates. Toscanini, who conducted both works, did not greatly admire them, finding the* verismo *movement rather common in both literary and musical style.*

The end of the nineteenth century was a time of difficult transition for Italian music—that is to say, for opera. Giuseppe Verdi, though old and no longer very active, cast the shadow of a colossus across the path of young composers. Meanwhile, the influence of Richard Wagner was sweeping from the north into Italy. To avoid comparison with either of these giants, the new generation of composers embraced *scapigliatura*—"dishevelment," the hippie movement of the day. Bohemian in clothes and manners, they favored the *verismo* or realism of such writers as Balzac, Zola and the Sicilian Giovanni Verga, who described everyday life and ordinary people. Toscanini contributed to the success of *verismo* by conducting operas of its leading exponents, Pietro Mascagni and Ruggero Leoncavallo. But because of their raw, unpoetic librettos and sometimes commonplace music, these works did not especially appeal to Toscanini. His taste and loyalties inclined more toward his friend Alfredo Catalani, a serious, cosmopolitan composer.

Both personally and professionally, Toscanini faced problems of his own. His father, never provident, trusting to luck, had gone into debt, and Arturo had to borrow money to help him. Thanks to his prodigious power of memorizing, Toscanini was now in demand to conduct or help prepare new works, such as Alberto Franchetti's *Cristoforo Colombo*, commissioned by the city of Genoa for the 400th anniversary of Columbus' voyage. He was having success, but his intransigence was creating obstacles. The Palermo season in late 1892, for instance, brought unfavorable reviews and a contretemps with the audience over his refusal to allow encores in Mascagni's *Cavalleria Rusticana*. Since the opera is based on a Sicilian story, the public may have felt a proprietary interest in it—and local newspaper accounts hinted darkly that Toscanini had offended powerful local figures. He left with a bitter taste in his mouth, never to work again in Palermo. The following summer in Milan, a heavier blow fell: the death of Catalani. Visiting his friend's bedside, Toscanini knew that the neglected composer, one of the first to help in his career, now depended on him in return, to carry the flickering torch for his operas into an uncertain future.

The widely heralded premiere in Genoa in 1892 of a new opera marking the 400th anniversary of Christopher Columbus' voyage of discovery to the New World (poster at left), music by Alberto Franchetti (below left), enlisted Toscanini as assistant to Luigi Mancinelli (middle left). Seldom revived today, Franchetti's operas once enjoyed a vogue.

Toscanini's preference among newer operas fell to his friend Alfredo Catalani (below right), whose death in 1893 deeply grieved him. Despite Toscanini's advocacy, the public did not warm lastingly to Catalani, preferring the short, pithy Cavalleria and Pagliacci (score, poster at foot). Center of page: Giovanni Verga, author of Cavalleria story.

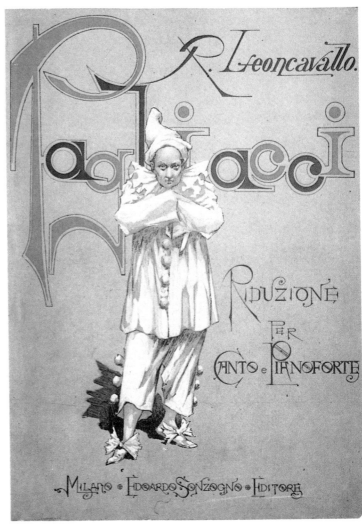

Though Milan always has been the capital of Italian musical life, the city of Turin, not far away, became a rival when it established its own symphony orchestra in 1894. Design of poster below combines a classic theme, an appeal to the traditional role of the muses, with a timely look, a premonition of the Art Nouveau style soon to flower all over Europe.

Toscanini, lower left, sporting the jaunty hat he wore so often, posed in a businesslike suit for his Turin portrait. He was invited to form and lead the new orchestra, which also would give opera performances at the city's Teatro Regio. Guiding light of the project was Giuseppe Depanis, lower right, farsighted city father who was also a writer on musical subjects.

X. TWO MAJOR ENGAGEMENTS

The death of his friend Alfredo Catalani in the summer of 1893 coincided with a slack period in Toscanini's career. But in 1894 engagements picked up again. In Brescia he took his mother along to cook for him, saving on expenses. In Treviso for the first time he conducted Verdi's *Falstaff*, which had had its premiere only a year before. Though a connoisseur's piece, never a prime favorite with the general public, *Falstaff* was the opera Toscanini would conduct most often in his life. In Pisa he created a stir by firing two-thirds of the orchestra, whose remaining colleagues went on strike in their defense. The local prefect, called in to arbitrate, said the fired players should be paid, but Toscanini was allowed to send for replacements.

The following year brought him closer to his goal of a permanent job. Civic pride in Turin was behind it: home of Italy's royal family, the Piedmontese city was disappointed not to have been made the nation's capital. Giuseppe Depanis, a farsighted lawyer, city councilor and music critic, invited Toscanini to set up a municipal orchestra, which also would form the basis of an opera company. It was a revolutionary idea—neither Milan nor Rome had a permanent orchestra at the time—and Toscanini seized the opportunity to present at the Teatro Regio the Italian premiere of Wagner's *Götterdämmerung*, guaranteed to draw national attention.

Another engagement awaited Toscanini: matrimony. Though they did not actually marry until two years later, it was in Turin that he met Carla De Martini, eighteen, sister of Ida, who played a Rhinemaiden in *Götterdämmerung*. These two were from an established middle-class Milan family, daughters of an investment banker. Ida in turn would marry Toscanini's violinist friend Enrico Polo, concertmaster of the new orchestra.

When the next production, *Falstaff*, went into rehearsal, Toscanini showed his usual attention to every detail, noticing that the choristers' shoes were not of the right period. Arrigo Boito, the poet who wrote the *Falstaff* libretto, became friendly with him. So did Giacomo Puccini, who accepted the young man as conductor of the world premiere of his next opera in Turin. Milan now had a rival city for musical eminence.

The Teatro Regio of Turin, whose stage is shown at left, now became the scene of ambitious opera projects staged by Toscanini, while his symphony concert series (program below) offered such novelties as the Italian premiere of three of Verdi's Quattro Pezzi Sacri (Four Sacred Pieces). Though Verdi did not attend, he heard favorable reports from Arrigo Boito.

In the environs of Turin the busy Maestro found time for a favorite escape, mountain hiking, joined by the De Martini sisters (lower left), Ida and Carla—the latter soon his fiancée, the former to wed his Parma schoolmate, violinist Enrico Polo. Gamboling at Groscavallo, lower right: Polo (with mustache), sculptor Leonardo Bistolfi (with beard), Toscanini.

Esposizione Generale Italiana in Torino 1898

Programma Illustrato

DEL

SESTO CONCERTO

Vocale ed Istrumentale

PRIMA ESECUZIONE IN ITALIA
di tre pezzi Sacri di GIUSEPPE VERDI
(Proprietà di G. Ricordi e Co)

GIOVEDÌ 26 MAGGIO, ALLE ORE 21 PRECISE
nel GRANDE SALONE

Cent. 20.

TORINO
TIPOGRAFIA ROUX FRASSATI & Co
1898.

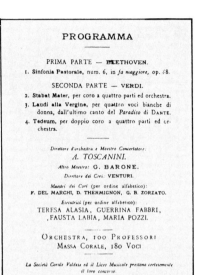

PROGRAMMA

PRIMA PARTE — BEETHOVEN.

1. Sinfonia Pastorale, num. 6, in *fa maggiore*, op. 68.

SECONDA PARTE — VERDI.

2. Stabat Mater, per coro a quattro parti ed orchestra.
3. Laudi alla Vergine, per quattro voci bianche di donna, dall'ultimo canto del *Paradiso* di DANTE.
4. Tedeum, per doppio coro a quattro parti ed orchestra.

Direttore d'orchestra e Maestro Concertatore:
A. TOSCANINI.
Altro Maestro: G. BARONE.
Direttore dei Cori: VENTURI.

Maestri dei Cori (per ordine alfabetico):
F. DEL MARCHI, D. THERMIGNON, G. B. ZORZATO.

Esecutrici (per ordine alfabetico):
TERESA ALASIA, GUERRINA FABBRI, FAUSTA LABIA, MARIA POZZI.

ORCHESTRA, 100 PROFESSORI
MASSA CORALE, 180 VOCI

La Società Corale Valdese ed il Liceo Musicale prestano cortesemente il loro concorso.

The painting of Giacomo Puccini shown below captures the debonair spirit embodied in La Bohème—*one of three world premieres by Puccini that Toscanini conducted, the others being* La Fanciulla del West *(1910) and* Turandot *(1924). Only in* La Bohème *(1896) did the composer treat a subject directly identifiable with his own life.*

In the original-cast photos shown here, starting with Act I at the foot of the page, Evan Gorga is Rodolfo, Cesira Ferrani the Mimì. Live-performance photography was unknown at the time, but through the posed quality of these postcards it is possible to sense the novelty with which a relatively modern subject was put onstage, the singers acting naturally.

Puccini's new opera, *La Bohème*, was the most important world premiere Toscanini had yet conducted. In line with *verismo*, the "new realism," it told a modern story, in costumes of recent period, with poor young artists as its protagonists and informal, even risqué subject matter, including free love. Puccini was not wholly committed to *verismo*, however, and the flights of melodic poetry in his work are what have made it last. He and Toscanini chose young singers who would be convincing in their roles. Puccini's publisher, Giulio Ricordi, promoted the production shrewdly. After the premiere on February 1, 1896, the critical press was divided, but the public was enthusiastic, and four extra performances had to be scheduled.

As the spring approached, Toscanini made his first appearance as a symphony conductor (March 20), choosing a program of unfamiliar music, including the Italian premiere of Brahms' *Tragic Overture*. Though Toscanini continued to lead operas in other cities from time to time, his work in Turin carried forward. For the Teatro Regio he chose Wagner's demanding *Tristan und Isolde*. When performing *La Bohème* he had the houselights dimmed, taking a cue from Wagner's practice at the Bayreuth Festival. This was the first time such a thing had been done in Italy, and when he tried to repeat it for *Tristan*, a longer opera, there were protests, settled by lowering the lights halfway.

At the beginning of summer the next year, on June 21, 1897, Toscanini and Carla De Martini were married—he thirty, she close to twenty. To avoid publicity, they chose an out-of-the-way rural place for the wedding, but word leaked out, drawing curiosity-seekers. With his dislike of surprises or any nonmusical attention, Toscanini took the intrusion badly, withdrawing into a black mood. Nevertheless, the couple's first child, Walter, named after the hero of Catalani's *Loreley*, was born nine months later to the day, on March 21, 1898. It became a family joke that just once in his life Walter had been on time. *La Bohème* went on to become a world success, but for Puccini and Toscanini, the Bohemian life was a thing of the past. Both were now family men, and in the limelight of the Italian musical scene.

The first performance of La Bohème *took place in Turin, rather than the more obvious choice of Milan, partly because Puccini wanted Toscanini to conduct, partly because the publisher Giulio Ricordi, a shrewd publicist, wanted to create a special occasion. The cast, listed on the poster at left, was made up of young actors who looked their parts.*

Below left, two more simulated scenes from the opera—the Act III quartet and Mimì's death at the end of Act IV. Puccini and Toscanini directed the staging themselves, having coached the singers in the desired musical delivery. At right below, hand-tinted portrait photos of Toscanini and his bride dating from the time of their marriage.

Count Guido Visconti di Modrone (left) was head of the board of directors at La Scala when his vice president, composer-poet-librettist Arrigo Boito (right), proposed two young men, Arturo Toscanini and Giulio Gatti-Casazza, to run the theater. It was a risky move, considering Toscanini's volatility, but an inspired one, considering his high standards and energy.

Having engineered Toscanini's appointment, Boito wrote a letter (bottom) to the conductor, telling him the choice would fall on him. Boito further volunteered advice on how to choose musicians for the orchestra—the theater's first permanent one in its history—and how to negotiate terms with the board of directors when accepting the offer.

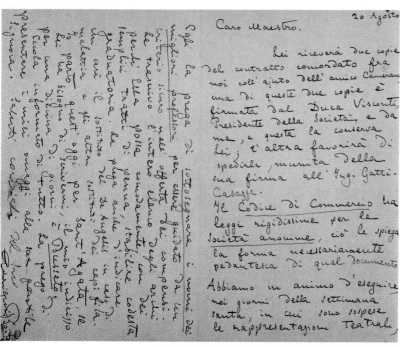

The Teatro alla Scala in Milan has always represented the pinnacle of Italian opera. But it has not always upheld its reputation. Verdi turned his back on it for many years. With the premieres of his two final operas, *Otello* and *Falstaff*, Verdi made peace with La Scala, and the librettist of those operas, Arrigo Boito, was now vice president of its board of directors, headed by an enlightened patron of the arts, Duke Guido Visconti di Modrone. It was Boito who put forward the names of Arturo Toscanini and Giulio Gatti-Casazza for a reorganized artistic and business administration of the theater. Some board members felt, with reason, that Toscanini's disposition might not be conducive to harmonious management. They also questioned whether Gatti-Casazza had enough experience.

Toscanini's musical qualifications were not open to question. In twelve years he had led 113 productions of fifty-eight operas all over Italy. When the reorganization of La Scala was announced in June 1898 and he was invited to take over, he insisted on full control over repertory, choice of performers, stage design, rehearsal and performance schedules. Surprisingly, these terms were accepted, and while continuing his concert series with the Turin orchestra, he held meetings with La Scala officials to plan the season. The traditional opening date, December 26, was the occasion of Wagner's *Die Meistersinger*, which required extra preparation. (Operas were not rotated in repertory but were, and still are, presented one at a time for several performances each, the so-called *stagione* system.) With the second opera, Bellini's *Norma*, the board found that Toscanini meant what he said. Exercising his authority, he canceled the performance after the dress rehearsal: he was not satisfied with it. When a compromise was suggested—an assistant conductor could lead *Norma* in his place—Toscanini replied he was responsible for the standards of everything at La Scala. This left a six-opera season, equally divided between familiar works and novelties. To avoid distractions, the house was darkened, and ladies' hats were no longer permitted on the parquet level, where they would obstruct visibility. The old drop curtain was replaced with a side-opening curtain. A revolution had begun.

Cartoon from the humorous magazine Guerin Meschino *(left) shows newly appointed manager Gatti-Casazza pointing out features of repertory and roster on season's billboard outside La Scala while Visconti (with beard), Ricordi (at right) and Toscanini (with hat) look on. Tall man in center background is Visconti's son, Duke Uberto.*

In lower cartoon, Toscanini and Gatti-Casazza take to the telephone in their roundup of artists for the new regime. La Scala, little changed today (auditorium at bottom), remains the mecca of Italian opera. While Toscanini was taking over, his first child, Walter (birth announcement below) was born in Turin and named after hero of Catalani's Loreley.

27

Toscanini's friend and champion, Arrigo Boito, was also the librettist for the last two operas of Giuseppe Verdi, Otello *and* Falstaff, *both based on Shakespeare. Below, the two men stand together outside Verdi's villa, Sant'Agata, around 1890. Though Toscanini had met with Verdi on several occasions, his contacts with the old composer were rather limited.*

Because Verdi led a secluded life in his latter years and seldom went to performances, he had to rely on reports from people he trusted. From Giulio Ricordi he gathered an opinion of Toscanini as something of an autocrat. But hearing from Boito how well Toscanini had put on Falstaff *at La Scala, the master sent a telegram of thanks (bottom).*

XIII. TRIALS OF A NONCONFORMIST

Arturo Toscanini's forthright, independent manner set him apart from other musicians. Because he gave his utmost and expected colleagues to give theirs, he was judged a slave driver by those more willing to compromise. And though usually courteous in social relations, he often expressed himself bluntly on the podium, resorting to frustrated abuse when angry. His emergence as artistic arbiter of Italy's principal opera house at a relatively youthful age was guaranteed to arouse controversy.

An early adversary was the powerful Giulio Ricordi, publisher of Verdi and Puccini. Accustomed to controlling which operas were staged in what theaters, with what singers and scenic designs, Ricordi found Toscanini uncooperative. He also suspected him of being a Wagnerite—a suspicion fueled by Toscanini's first visit to Germany in 1899, accompanied by Gatti-Casazza, to find out how Wagner's operas were staged in the mother country. The publisher relayed his dissatisfaction to Verdi, who replied regretting the present-day "tyranny of the conductors." But Arrigo Boito, who also had Verdi's ear, was giving the old composer a more favorable report on Toscanini. Meanwhile, Ricordi's newspaper, the *Gazzetta Musicale di Milano*, kept a critical eye on the young iconoclast.

While this reaction cannot have pleased Toscanini, he must have expected it. He had not gone out of his way to cultivate Ricordi, who after all was a man of the past, representing much that Toscanini wanted to change in Italian habits of opera production. Deeply respecting Verdi, he would have preferred to discuss his ideas directly with the composer, but access to Verdi was controlled by Ricordi. Toscanini's attitude, then and throughout his life, was that his work should speak for itself. There was no point in trying to persuade anyone except by direct proof—the results to be seen on the stage. In any event, he had taken on a full-time job that left little time for social niceties or parliamentary intrigues. The theater demanded and received from him more time and fuller attention than from anyone else. His family often said goodbye to him at breakfast and did not see him again until after that night's performance. Toscanini was an indefatigable worker, and his workplace was the theater.

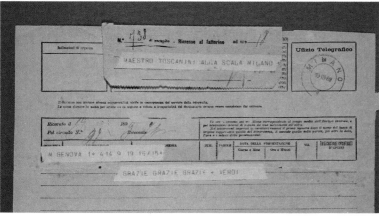

Verdi's publisher, Giulio Ricordi (left), something of a tyrant in his own right, mistrusted the "tyranny of the conductors." In his view, it was the publisher who should control the repertory and casting of the opera houses. Yet a courteous if brief note (bottom left), always carried by Toscanini thereafter, showed Verdi's appreciation of the young conductor.

Alongside Verdi in Toscanini's pantheon was Wagner, whose works often opened his seasons at La Scala. Still quite a novelty in Italy, they posed a challenge to the theatrical machinery and techniques of the day. Below, Giuseppe Borgatti, a convincing figure for Siegfried in his forging scene. Bottom, the forest scene of Siegfried, as seen at La Scala.

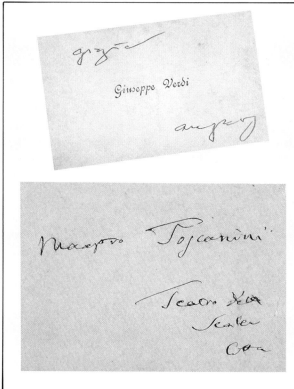

Intensely devoted to his family, Toscanini carried a sort of reliquary with portraits of his children and wife (below), keeping it on his dressing-room table at the theater. Nevertheless, for a time he became amorously involved with the soprano Rosina Storchio, a gifted interpreter who often figured in performances he led at La Scala and in South America.

Storchio sang (but Toscanini did not conduct) the disastrous premiere of Puccini's **Madama Butterfly** at La Scala in 1908, after which she often sang the role of the geisha in other theaters but refused to repeat it in Milan. At bottom, she is shown with the elegant baritone Giuseppe De Luca, another of Toscanini's preferred artists, in Donizetti's **Don Pasquale**.

All his life, Arturo Toscanini was a family man. He had no use for divorce: one wife, one husband, was enough. Yet according to theater conventions, romantic liaisons were tolerated so long as they did not spill over into "polite" society or poison one's domestic relations. Perhaps naively, Toscanini believed that the family and one's outside romantic life could be kept separate. He loved and appreciated attractive women, and often the feeling was mutual. He pursued them with the same energy that he brought to his work.

In January 1900 his daughter Wally was born, named after the protagonist of Catalani's opera *La Wally*. Preparing the world premiere of Leoncavallo's *Zaza* at the Teatro Lirico in Milan in November of that year, Toscanini discovered the allure of Rosina Storchio, who sang the title role. It was not long before he was involved in an affair—one of the most serious of Toscanini's liaisons, though it ended before 1915, when he and Storchio made their last professional appearances together.

Meanwhile, Toscanini's wife gave birth to another child, Giorgio, in September 1901. She suffered her husband's philandering in silence. Toscanini the devoted paterfamilias, who enjoyed playing with his children at home, seems not to have let the stresses of his emotional life interfere with his first love, music. Among his innovations at La Scala was the separation of ballet evenings from opera evenings. Before, even for so important an event as the premiere of *Otello* or *Falstaff*, a ballet followed. His third La Scala season was to have opened with *Tristan und Isolde*, but the tenor's illness forced replacement with *La Bohème*—coolly received, despite a promising new tenor, Enrico Caruso. *Tristan* finally went on at the end of December 1900, with side lighting arranged to the conductor's specifications.

On January 27, 1901, Giuseppe Verdi died at the Hotel de Milan at the age of eighty-seven. A month later, when burial took place at the Casa di Riposo—the home for retired musicians that Verdi had founded in Milan—Toscanini conducted the chorus and orchestra of La Scala in a final tribute, "Va, pensiero" from *Nabucco*, in the chilly square outside the Cimetero Monumentale, the temporary resting place from which Verdi's body was moved.

At left, a rare photo of Enrico Caruso as *Rodolfo* in **La Bohème**, taken by a Russian photographer in St. Petersburg around the time the tenor also sang the role at La Scala. Below left, Enrico Polo, Toscanini's brother-in-law, with the Maestro and their first sons. Toscanini wore the beard briefly, after sunburn from a glacier's glare during mountain hiking.

As artistic director of La Scala, Toscanini led the theater's chorus and orchestra in "Va, pensiero" from Nabucco—an anthem of the Risorgimento—at Verdi's public funeral observance in 1901 (below). Bottom, Cosima Wagner's letter of thanks after learning of **Tristan** production from her son Siegfried, shown with her later (right) on the streets of Bayreuth.

Many Italians emigrated to South as well as North America, spreading their love of opera. After his unscheduled debut there in 1885, Toscanini visited South America six more times, starting in 1901, when Caruso sang his only Lohengrin—in Italian (program at left). For the 1906 season in Buenos Aires, program cover (right) showed an allegory of Music.

In 1908 the old Teatro de la Opera in Buenos Aires (below left) was replaced by the much larger Teatro Colón (bottom). Ettore Panizza, an Italo-Argentine (below right), later became a strong collaborator of Toscanini's on the conducting staff at La Scala and enjoyed a distinguished career at the Metropolitan Opera in New York during the seasons 1934-42.

XV. BUENOS AIRES

When Toscanini returned in 1901 to South America, scene of his impromptu debut fifteen years earlier, he came back as a well-known artistic figure. Once again the troupe included prominent soloists—the tenor Enrico Caruso was among them, ready to hazard his only Lohengrin (in Italian)—and the repertory included *Aida*, the work that had catapulted Toscanini to the podium for the first time. But on this visit the conductor's passion for Wagner was in evidence. Not only the fairly familiar *Lohengrin* and *Tannhäuser* but the more difficult and novel *Tristan und Isolde* were on the bill.

In contrast to the close-fitting schedules of performers in today's age of the jet airplane, the season, which ran from mid-May to mid-September (Argentina's winter months), was leisurely and relaxed, with a long ocean voyage at either end. For audiences in Buenos Aires and Montevideo, Uruguay, where some performances also were given, these extended seasons offered a link with European cultural life. Many Italians and other Europeans, as Toscanini knew from his first visit, had settled in South America, where cities were being built on European models. The Teatro de la Opera in Buenos Aires could offer a run of operas comparable in length to La Scala's own series, with some of the same stars. The repertory included operas not yet heard in Argentina: besides *Tristan*, there were Berlioz' *Damnation de Faust*, Catalani's *La Wally*,

Left, a cartoonist sketched the seated Maestro during one of his Latin American sojourns. Even so far along in his career, apparently, he did not always stand to conduct in the orchestra pit, especially when rehearsing. Below, a local photographer captured Toscanini with his wife among a crowd of strollers outside the park in Buenos Aires in 1906.

Lower picture, a dockside scene, shows a transatlantic ship preparing for departure. Toscanini's tours arrived and returned home on such ships. The Teatro Colón as it appears today, bottom left, adjoins a street renamed after Toscanini, in whose honor a plaque (bottom right) also has been attached to the outside of the building.

Puccini's *Madama Butterfly* and several others less familiar, such as *Medio Evo Latino* by Argentine-born Ettore Panizza, a composer-conductor who became one of Toscanini's right-hand men at La Scala and in 1934-42 had a distinguished period of conducting at the Metropolitan Opera in New York.

Toscanini's career in Buenos Aires was substantial. He went there in 1901, 1903, 1904, 1906, 1912, in 1940 with the NBC Symphony and in 1941 to lead the Teatro Colón orchestra. During the first four of these visits, performances were staged at the Teatro de la Opera. In 1912 and for the 1940-41 concerts, the more spacious Teatro Colón, inaugurated in 1908, was available. After Toscanini's death, the street next to the Teatro Colón was renamed for him, and a commemorative plaque was placed on the façade of the building.

One of Toscanini's most important hopes for La Scala was to replace the old parquet-level orchestra seating (below) with a sunken pit, inspired by the wholly submerged pit under the stage at Wagner's Bayreuth Festival House, shown at bottom of page. Though orchestra pits are universally accepted now, Toscanini's plan caused a furor.

In fact the conductor did not find any of his reforms easy going, especially after the board of directors was taken over by the rather unsympathetic Uberto (left), son of the deceased Count Guido Visconti. To free Toscanini for the theater's artistic problems, his wife, Carla (right), took care of the household and finances: the Maestro rarely carried money.

XVI. BREAK WITH LA SCALA

The 1902-03 season brought disruption in Arturo Toscanini's relations with La Scala. Dissatisfaction with his reforms had been growing—yet these were far from complete. For example, despite his reluctance to grant encores, at this stage in his career he still allowed them. It was an altercation over an encore demanded by the audience at the last performance of the season, Verdi's *Un Ballo in Maschera*, that precipitated Toscanini's departure. He left in a fury at the end of the first act, and an assistant, Pietro Sormani, finished the performance. Arriving home, Toscanini told his wife he was finished with La Scala. Early the next morning he left, as scheduled, for another season in Buenos Aires.

With the death of Duke Guido Visconti di Modrone in 1902, La Scala lost a progressive, artistically principled leader. The new management, under the Duke's son Uberto, started to pinch pennies. Though Toscanini was never one to think in terms of money, he realized—or had been made aware by his wife, who handled the finances—that his salary was low in proportion to what the singers were earning, or to what Buenos Aires was paying him. When he asked for a raise, La Scala tried to compromise, making him feel unappreciated. With the prospect of continued opposition to his reforms, it was time to move on.

In those five seasons, Toscanini had wrought deep changes, not only in the structure and function of the great theater but in the face of opera throughout Italy—and therefore of opera throughout the world. With little precedent to guide him, he had followed his artistic conscience. Fate created him with the will and energy to implement his vision, though not so quickly or thoroughly as he would have liked. Under pressure from Toscanini, La Scala had built a permanent orchestra of the best players in Italy. Rehearsal schedule and casting had been revised to allow for painstaking preparation. To achieve such high standards had been the dream of serious dramatists, notably Wagner, who created the Bayreuth Festival to realize his goals. It was the age-old struggle of music as a social event versus music as art. To reach these ends meant going against entrenched custom, and it demanded strength and perseverance.

Toscanini, whose love for Verdi never conflicted with his passion for Wagner, continued to play the German master's works in abundance at La Scala. Popular illustrations of the period, inspired by La Scala, show the aesthetic in which Siegfried *(middle left, with dragon, Act II) and* Lohengrin (bottom left, Elsa awaiting swan knight's arrival, Act I) *were staged.*

Scenic designs of the same era show how the first and second acts of Die Meistersinger *(right, top and bottom) looked at La Scala. But Toscanini's first period there came to an end with Verdi: the poster at left announces* Un Ballo in Maschera, *during which he quit, having refused an encore neither he nor the tenor Giovanni Zenatello wanted to allow.*

Contemporary composers whose works Toscanini introduced to Italy: below left, the Russian master Piotr Ilyich Tchaikovsky, whose Romeo and Juliet *Overture and* Pathétique *Symphony figured on many a later Toscanini program. Right, Johannes Brahms, with eighteen-year-old Henriette Hemala at the home of the Miller zu Aichholz family at Gmunden.*

Lower left, Finland's Jean Sibelius, leader of Scandinavian National Romanticism, whose tone poems En Saga *and* Swan of Tuonela *arrived in Italy via Toscanini in Turin. Lower right, Richard Strauss, composer of the opera* Salome, *object of Toscanini's struggle to give the Italian premiere in Milan while Strauss himself wanted to do so in Turin.*

XVII. SPREADING CAREER IN ITALY

Toscanini had left his mark on the symphony orchestra of Turin and the opera company of Milan. But in 1903, when he left La Scala, he was beginning over again. Not every orchestra or opera company that he was invited to conduct had risen above a provincial standard. Returning to Turin for concerts, he presented novelties from abroad—*En Saga* by Sibelius, the *Enigma* Variations by Elgar, *L'Après-midi d'un Faune* by Debussy, all classics today but "modern music" at that time.

At La Scala, Toscanini's place was taken by Cleofonte Campanini, son of the blacksmith who had accompanied Claudio Toscanini to the birth registry after Arturo was born. Audiences appreciated Campanini's ability but soon started to miss the excitement and intensity of the Toscanini whose reforms they had resisted. During this period of free-lance conducting, meanwhile, Toscanini emerged as a tireless leader of orchestra tours, a role in which he would excel throughout his life. Even large cities at that time had not yet heard the likes of the Turin orchestra, with which he traveled to Milan, Venice, Parma, Trieste, Brescia and Como. Radio broadcasts did not exist, and phonograph records were in an embryonic state. Such tours spread the gospel of concert music through a land conditioned primarily to opera. Toscanini took his missionary role seriously, introducing music by composers still little-known in Italy—Berlioz, Dvořák, Tchaikovsky, Brahms.

This schedule of constant touring did not augur well for a musician's home life. Toscanini's wife and children accompanied him when possible; when only his wife could come, the children were left with Eugenia ("Nena") Rama, a governess who stayed with the family for her lifetime and was buried in their tomb. The children were disciplined by their mother and Nena, leaving their father free to appear a hero to his offspring. By now a man of some means, he started to collect contemporary paintings and enjoyed the company of literary and artistic friends. But mainly his energy was needed to sustain long periods of work. He seldom carried money: his wife took care of life's day-to-day details. On tour, there must have been days when he longed for the comforts of home.

Bohemian composer Antonín Dvořák, left, inscribed his photo with the theme of his Symphonic Variations, *a favorite with Toscanini. Below, the young conductor in boater hat and wife (left foreground) pose with friends, nurses (family governess Nena Rama at right) and young children. Despite pastoral setting, the Maestro as usual is nattily dressed.*

Below, Toscanini with priest composer Don Lorenzo Perosi, whose oratorio The Resurrection of Lazarus *was given at La Scala in the spring of 1899. Bottom (from left), Toscanini brought Italy works by Engelbert Humperdinck (Caruso caricature), Sir Edward Elgar and Jules Massenet (also by Caruso), while Cleofonte Campanini (right) replaced Toscanini at Scala.*

The Toscaninis' second son, Giorgio (left), died in June 1906 of diphtheria during South American opera tour, aged four and a half. Three months earlier, the family patriarch, the conductor's father, Claudio (right), died in Milan and was laid to rest wearing his prized red shirt, uniform of those who fought with Garibaldi for Italian independence.

The youngest and oldest, they lie buried in the Cimitero Monumentale of Milan in the family plot, where the Toscanini tomb (bottom), incised with bas-reliefs, was designed by sculptor Leonardo Bistolfi. A friend from the days in Turin, Bistolfi was one of the conductor's many contacts with the visual arts, in which he maintained a lively interest.

In March 1906, Toscanini's father, Claudio, died at seventy-three, a free spirit and a Garibaldi republican to the last. He was buried in his red shirt, which he had worn to reunions of the *garibaldini*: once considered "irregulars" and roughnecks, they now were honored veterans of the struggle for a free Italy. It seemed a dark shadow was passing over the family, for in June, during another South American season, the Toscaninis' youngest child, Giorgio, died of diphtheria in Buenos Aires, not yet five years old. Despite strains on the marriage, the relationship of Arturo nd Carla Toscanini survived this difficult period, and eighteen months later their daughter Wanda was born.

Meanwhile, Toscanini had important career decisions to face. Asked by La Scala to return to the Milanese theater, he seized the opportunity to insist on his conditions: the rule against encores must be enforced consistently, there should be no interference from outsiders at rehearsals, and a pit should be built for the orchestra. (Until that time, it was customary for the orchestra to sit on the parquet level, separated from the audience only by a railing.) The influential publisher Giulio Ricordi, still viewing Toscanini as an upstart Wagnerophile, opposed the construction of the pit and ran a cartoon showing the players being lowered in by a derrick.

Having agreed to return to La Scala, Toscanini found himself at odds with the German composer Richard Strauss. While still in Turin, Toscanini had asked for the rights to the Italian premiere of Strauss' new opera *Salome*; now that he was back in Milan, he felt the idea had been his and he was still entitled to priority. Meanwhile, Strauss had signed to conduct the work himself in Turin for a lucrative fee. Journeying to Berlin to confront Strauss, Toscanini uttered his famous epigram "As a musician I take my hat off to you—as a man I *put on seven hats!*" (accompanied, as he told the story years later, by vigorous gestures of putting on the hats). In the end, Toscanini led his own production at La Scala, detracting from the publicity for Strauss' simultaneous performance in Turin. Though the composer twenty years later tried to conciliate him by sending an autographed page of *Salome*, the two never became personal friends.

At left, Salomea Krusceniska (also known as Krusceniski) in her namesake role of Salome, which the soprano sang in Toscanini's Milan production of the Strauss opera. Below left, Maestro holds his youngest child, Wanda, born in Milan in 1907. After the death of Giorgio, the children were given names starting with the letter "W," presumed lucky.

Cartoon (below) depicts contre-temps between "Tossecanina" (whooping cough) conductor and Richard Strauss, drawn as a sly cat, over which of them would introduce Salome in Italy. Silver platter on which Salome received head of John the Baptist supplied theme for conductor's souvenir tray, bottom, etched with likeness of the Biblical siren.

Giulio Gatti-Casazza and wife, soprano Frances Alda, accompanied Toscanini in 1908 to Metropolitan Opera, where Gatti would serve as general manager until 1935.
Below the couple, Gustav Mahler (mid left), who preceded Toscanini to the Met after heading the Court Opera in Vienna. Toscanini held Mahler in respect as a conductor if not as a composer.

Middle right, Heinrich Conried, a former actor, who preceded Gatti as general manager and engaged Mahler to conduct at the Met. Bottom, financiers Otto Kahn, August Belmont, admirers of Toscanini after encountering his work at La Scala; their opinions and decisions wielded heavy influence on the board of directors of the Metropolitan Opera at that time.

Toscanini's return to La Scala lasted two seasons. For the first of these, 1906-07, in addition to the novelty of *Salome*, he continued his loyalty and admiration for Wagner, Verdi and Catalani. To inaugurate the new orchestra pit the following season he chose Wagner's *Götterdämmerung*. Problems with the public, however, were not long in coming. Charpentier's *Louise*, a foreign novelty, was not appreciated, though it introduced a New Zealand soprano of uncommon quality, Frances Alda. In her memoirs Alda recalled going through the entire role with a rehearsal pianist, only to have Toscanini ask, "In what language were you singing?" Soon, as wife of Toscanini's managerial colleague Giulio Gatti-Casazza, she would emerge as a major figure in the New York careers of the two men. During the season, it was announced that both would be leaving to join the Metropolitan Opera.

The Met had been trying to engage Toscanini since 1903. One of the company's most influential backers, the financier Otto H. Kahn, had heard Toscanini conduct in Italy and was determined to engage him. Meanwhile, the general manager, Heinrich Conried, who had approached Toscanini first, had to step down for health reasons, and the board of directors offered his job to Gatti-Casazza. Convinced that the Met was a serious theater with high standards, Toscanini and Gatti-Casazza reached an agreement with the board of directors—something they were finding increasingly difficult to do at La Scala.

Resentment on the part of the Milanese public interfered with Toscanini's aims for the remainder of his 1907-08 La Scala season. Though some hailed it, the public disliked Debussy's *Pelléas et Mélisande*. When hecklers sarcastically called out "Che bella musica!," Toscanini turned and shouted back, "Si, si, per me, bella musica!" Though Toscanini and Gatti-Casazza were not close, always treating each other somewhat formally, they had worked out a practicable relationship in the theater, one that would endure fourteen years. When they boarded ship in the fall of 1908, one era had ended and another, in the New World, was about to begin. The Metropolitan Opera, like La Scala, would never be the same again.

Left, poster for Debussy's Pelléas et Mélisande, *introduced to Italy by Toscanini at La Scala, where its impressionism and conversational style vexed many; the composer's portrait superimposed. Below, the Neapolitan tenor Enrico Caruso with the Maestro around the time of their first season together at the Metropolitan, which opened with Caruso in* Aida.

Bottom left, Caruso's caricature of Gustave Charpentier, composer of Louise, *performed at La Scala and the Met. Directly below, his sketch of Toscanini conducting a rehearsal at the New York theater. Bottom, the two in a group onstage with choristers, stage personnel and other cast members after rehearsing double bill of* Le Villi *and* Cavalleria Rusticana *at Met.*

Alfred Hertz, left, conducted "German wing" at Metropolitan Opera while Toscanini headed Italian. Erstwhile tenor Andreas Dippel, right, was appointed to co-manage with Gatti-Casazza, but situation proved difficult and Dippel soon departed. Drawing of Met's top gallery shows enthusiastic immigrants who brought vitality to the opera audience.

At foot of page, a photograph of the Metropolitan Opera House during the 1908-09 season, when Toscanini and Gatti-Casazza arrived to take the artistic reins. Inaugurated in 1883 with Faust *in Italian under Cleofonte Campanini, the Met was first nicknamed the "yellow brick brewery," but city air eventually turned it very dark brown.*

XX. OFF TO NEW YORK

The arrival of Toscanini and Gatti-Casazza, together with the peak wave of Italian immigration to the New World, conspired to end the era of German domination that had endured at the Metropolitan Opera since the early 1890s. Yet this did not mean, as many feared, an Italian cultural takeover at the expense of German repertory. Toscanini opened his first season with *Aida* but asserted his versatility by preparing *Götterdämmerung*, finding errors in the orchestra parts that had been overlooked.

Unlike La Scala, which presented one opera at a time for several performances, the Met rotated several operas at once. Toscanini had to get used to this unfamiliar system, also to sharing the artistic leadership with Alfred Hertz and Gustav Mahler, who conducted the German wing. (The German and French/Italian wings had separate chorus and orchestra personnel.) Furthermore, the management obliged Gatti-Casazza to share managerial duties with Andreas Dippel, a former tenor, whom the established singers regarded as their advocate. It took two seasons before Dippel's plans for the company proved impracticable and Gatti-Casazza gained full control. Meanwhile, Toscanini's uncompromising manner produced the usual friction. One of the first operas presented was *Madama Butterfly*, and at a stage rehearsal, the exchange between Geraldine Farrar (the protagonist) and the conductor went something like this: "Maestro, you have to follow me—I am the star." "Madam, the stars are in heaven. Here on earth there are only good and bad artists, and you are a bad artist." "Well, the public pays to see my face, not your back!" Toscanini had been asking the soprano to sing full voice, not to "mark" half-voice in the German manner.

To show the Met's achievements, the board of directors sent some of its stars for a month-long season at the Théâtre du Châtelet in Paris in late spring 1910. Rehearsing for the French premiere of *Manon Lescaut*, the visiting composer Giacomo Puccini playfully splashed a cup of espresso coffee on the expensive costume of Lucrezia Bori to make her look disheveled for the final scene. And Claude Debussy, who came to a rehearsal, told Toscanini he felt he was hearing the subtle coloration of the *Aida* prelude for the first time.

The big Czech tenor Leo Slezak on shipboard with Toscanini en route to the 1909-10 Met season, when he made his company debut as Verdi's Otello under the Maestro. At right, the auditorium of the old Met as it looked in later years with the triumphal scene of Aida onstage. This was the opera of Toscanini's own debut with the company on November 16, 1908.

The cast of Toscanini's Met debut included Emmy Destinn, Enrico Caruso, Louise Homer, Antonio Scotti and Adamo Didur, in group photo of triumphal scene, below left. Bottom: program, cartoon from spring 1910 visit by Met stars to Théâtre du Châtelet, Paris, where camera caught Toscanini and wife with daughter Wanda, Puccini and his son Tonio.

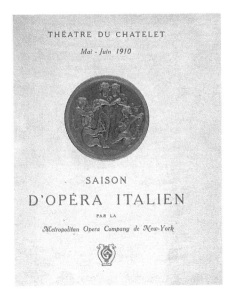

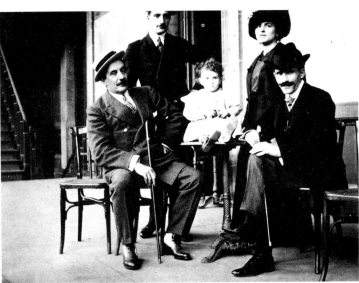

Major event in Metropolitan Opera history was world premiere of La Fanciulla del West *on December 10, 1910. Ticket prices were doubled. Below, general manager Gatti-Casazza with playwright David Belasco, who wrote original script (*The Girl of the Golden West*) and staged the opera, plus Toscanini (standing) and composer Puccini.*

Enrico Caruso, who sang the leading tenor role of the bandit Ramerrez, alias Nick Johnson, included himself (onstage at right) in his cartoon of a piano rehearsal. Toscanini, with arms outstretched, stands at the center of attention near the piano, while Belasco, Gatti-Casazza and Tito Ricordi, Puccini's publisher, are arranged from left onstage.

After the Met's visit to Paris, Toscanini went on to visit Puccini at Viareggio, the composer's home, to discuss his new opera, *La Fanciulla del West*, adapted from David Belasco's New York hit play *The Girl of the Golden West*. The Met had signed for the world premiere, and publicity was at fever pitch that November, when Puccini arrived in New York for rehearsals. He found the master showman Belasco trying to turn Caruso into an actor. (The leading soprano, Emmy Destinn, and the baritone villain, Pasquale Amato, were much more willing subjects.) The production set new standards for theatricality at the Met and consolidated the regime of Gatti-Casazza and Toscanini.

Each summer, Toscanini returned to Italy, and in this period he bought the house indelibly associated with him, at No. 20 Via Durini in Milan, a short

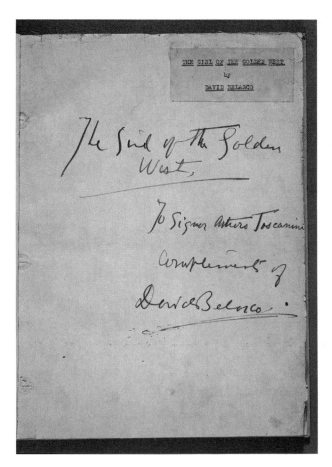

Belasco presented Toscanini with an autographed copy of the script of his original play, which had captured Puccini's imagination on his first U.S. trip (left). Below, Caruso with Emmy Destinn as the heroine, Minnie, in her mountainside cabin, where Act II takes place; at right is Marie Mattfeld as Wowkle, an Indian squaw, Minnie's housekeeper.

For the centenary of Verdi's birth, the little theater at Busseto, the town where the composer passed his early life, presented two of his operas, La Traviata and Falstaff, in the fall of 1913. Group picture shows Toscanini and Lucrezia Bori, front center, among other artists on front steps of the theater. At bottom, program announcement and poster.

walk from La Scala. He also revisited Turin, joining other well-known conductors for a concert series at the city's International Exposition. Maintaining a strenuous work schedule, he followed the next Met season with a trip to South America, where he conducted at the new Teatro Colón in Buenos Aires. For his 1912-13 season at the Met he led only revivals, except for Mussorgsky's *Boris Godunov*, which he introduced to the American public. As usual, he threw himself into every detail of staging and preparation. Before the next season began, he journeyed to Busseto, Verdi's hometown, to lead early fall performances of *La Traviata* and *Falstaff* in the town's little theater for the 100th anniversary of the composer's birth. Here, near Parma, where he had his own roots, Toscanini hoped to establish the tradition of a Verdi festival. In that same fall of 1913 he returned to La Scala after five years' absence to lead the *Messa da Requiem* and *Falstaff*.

The memory of Verdi was still in Toscanini's mind when he returned to the Met for 1913-14 with a galvanic revival of *Un Ballo in Maschera*. He also gave a nod to the new, introducing *L'Amore dei Tre Re* by thirty-eight-year-old Italo Montemezzi. Few in the audience for such successful evenings could suspect that Toscanini's years of glory at the Met were nearly at an end. Behind the scenes, however, forces were at work that would soon cause the history of La Scala to repeat itself in New York.

A focus of attention at the Met was the glamorous American soprano Geraldine Farrar, whose charms, personal as well as artistic, were not wasted on Toscanini. Though at first their personalities clashed, they worked together on many operas and became lovers, complicating the Maestro's family life and eventually contributing to his departure from the Met.

Farrar, shown below in the sort of clothes that kept her in the public eye, appears (bottom) in the throes of rehearsal for a world premiere in January 1915, Madame Sans-Gêne *by the verismo composer Umberto Giordano. With her in earnest conference on the stage set are Toscanini, who conducted the performance, and general manager Gatti-Casazza.*

XXII. BREAK WITH THE MET

"Kahn [financier Otto Kahn of the board of directors] has offered me a blank contract . . . but I shall not make any decision of the sort," noted Toscanini at the end of the Met's 1913-14 season. He did return for 1914-15, only to find his fears of a deteriorating situation increasingly justified. The Met did not permit him to institute a whole, consistent artistic policy. The management, even his old working mate Giulio Gatti-Casazza, still believed opera could be produced at a profit, cutting expenses where they believed it would not show—no extra stage musicians for *Un Ballo in Maschera*, local musicians for the *Aida* stage band in a tour city, an unrehearsed substitute stepping in as Escamillo for *Carmen*. In the growing atmosphere of a complacent status quo, Toscanini's striving toward betterment was striking a note of discord.

Meanwhile, Toscanini had become involved in an affair with the soprano Geraldine Farrar, who eventually insisted he choose between his family and her. But for Toscanini the idea of leaving his family was unthinkable. Artistically and personally, the situation was becoming unmanageable.

With the U.S. premiere of Boris Godunov *at the Met in March 1913, Toscanini fulfilled an ambition of many years. Sung in Italian in the Rimsky-Korsakov arrangement, with scenery designed by Alexandre Golovine for the Paris production by the Diaghilev company, the Mussorgsky opera featured Adamo Didur in the title role, at left with Léon Rothier.*

The last opera Toscanini presented before quitting the Met was Iris *by Mascagni. The program (below) shows by its wording— "under the direction of Arturo Toscanini"—that he now supervised the entire production, including staging. War in Europe, though Italy was not yet involved, hastened his departure, beset with dangers of travel (bottom).*

The Maestro's son Walter would recall years later with a laugh, "They say my father had such a bad disposition that he couldn't stay in any job longer than five years!" Even without the extenuating circumstance of his affair with Farrar, Toscanini probably would have left the Metropolitan Opera anyway on purely artistic grounds. He had insisted in vain to Otto Kahn, "Opera isn't supposed to make money, it's supposed to *lose* money!" This prophecy is accepted as inevitable today, but in 1915 the world was not ready for it. After several more exasperating incidents that convinced him artistic standards were slipping out of his grasp, Toscanini, increasingly concerned about the war in Europe (which Italy had not yet entered), canceled his last six performances and prepared to return home. In spite of tactful negotiations that continued into the following summer, he was not to be lured back. But luck stayed with him: had he not canceled and left early, he would have been aboard the *Lusitania*, sunk by a German torpedo on May 7, 1915. Shortly thereafter, Italy entered the war on the side of the Allies.

XXIII. WARTIME ITALY

Back in his homeland after his final break with the Metropolitan Opera, Toscanini busied himself with benefit programs to aid the war effort. There was an outdoor "monster concert"—one of few al fresco events he ever conducted—and an opera season at the Teatro Dal Verme in Milan to help musicians put out of work by the closing of other theaters. Musicians, not yet unionized, were among the forgotten men of World War I, when musical life came almost to a standstill. German music was officially banned in Rome after a disturbance caused by Toscanini's insistence on playing the "Forest Murmurs" from Wagner's *Siegfried*.

Toscanini, though he refused to surrender music to politics, had no hesitations as a patriot. His father, after all, had narrowly escaped death fighting for Italy's independence. Toscanini could not understand how Giacomo Puccini, caught in contract negotiations for an operetta to be performed in Vienna, could be so equivocal about breaking with the enemy. Several years of coolness resulted, and when the composer found that the traditional Christmas raisin cake had been sent to Toscanini in his name, he wired, "PANETTONE SENT BY MISTAKE STOP PUCCINI," to which the conductor wired back, "PANETTONE EATEN BY MISTAKE STOP TOSCANINI."

At fifty, Toscanini was past the age for military service but could still campaign musically at the front. Leading his own band for the soldiers, he was heard from a distance by his son Walter, an underage volunteer with the Arditi Alpini (mountain commandos) and an expert in wiping out machine-gun nests. Noting the precision of the playing, the young man thought, "If I didn't know better, I'd think that was Father conducting." Briefly reunited, the two went for a walk near enemy lines. Only the fact that they had to skirt a shell hole saved them from being decapitated by a stray piece of shrapnel that flew between them when they stepped apart.

After the war, the belligerent nations were devastated physically and economically. With the arts equally affected, the period up into 1920 was professionally fallow for Toscanini, who loved above all else to work. But reconstruction would come, and this reformer, who habitually built from the ground up, would have new challenges to face.

With the nightmare of war behind but the specter of lean times ahead, La Scala struggled back to its feet after the war. Among colleagues picked by Toscanini, as artistic director, were conductor Gino Marinuzzi (left) and administrator Angelo Scandiani (right), a former bass singer and electrical engineer, whose assistant was the tireless Anita Colombo.

Others on the staff were Antonino Votto (lower left), a trusted rehearsal assistant and staff conductor, and the chorus master Vittore Veneziani (lower right). Votto's career at La Scala lasted until his retirement in 1969. Veneziani, ousted by Fascists, was brought back at Toscanini's insistence when the theater opened again in 1946 after World War II.

During the war years, with many Italian theaters dark, the country's leading opera house went on with sporadic performances, some under distinguished maestros. But between the fall of 1913, when he had come as a guest for *Falstaff* in honor of Verdi's birth centennial, and November 1918, when he led *Mefistofele* as a memorial to the recently dead composer-poet Arrigo Boito, the name of Arturo Toscanini did not appear. When it finally resumed its place in the annals of La Scala in 1920, things had changed radically. The administrative council of La Scala accepted Toscanini's proposals for sweeping reform, appointing him "plenipotentiary director" with jurisdiction over everything.

From this point dates La Scala's modern status as an *ente autonomo*, i.e., a nonprofit corporation— no more stockholder/shareholder control. In effect the City of Milan gave the theater to itself. City money and open subscriptions, together with entertainment taxes and private donations, would support it. To begin, Toscanini formed an orchestra from the best players and took it on an arduous Italian tour for a little more than a month, then on an extended tour of the U.S. and Canada. The Metropolitan Opera, still hoping to lure Toscanini back, supported the tour and housed its opening concert. In Camden, New Jersey, near Philadelphia, at a church the Victor company used for a studio, Toscanini led the first recordings of his life, reorchestrating the pieces to suit the big acoustical horn. The group visited thirty-nine U.S. cities, plus Montreal and Toronto, for a total of sixty-eight concerts. Returning home in April 1921, it toured Italy further, reaching a final total of 133 concerts in eight months, heard by a quarter-million people.

La Scala's next golden age under Toscanini began with *Falstaff* in December 1921. The repertory also took contemporary works into account, introducing *Dèbora e Jaéle* by Ildebrando Pizzetti and *Sly* by Ermanno Wolf-Ferrari. Toscanini did not stint on familiar repertory but also asked his audience to pay attention to less frequently performed classics. Wagner, shunned during the war, was restored with *Die Meistersinger* and *Tristan und Isolde*. La Scala, newly reformed, took back its place as international leader among opera houses.

The long, arduous tour undertaken by the orchestra of La Scala began in Italy in November 1920, went on to U.S. and Canada (left, aboard ship with Toscanini). Mid-page: composers Ottorino Respighi (l.), whose symphonic works Toscanini introduced, and Ildebrando Pizzetti (r.), whose opera Dèbora e Jaéle (poster below) had its premiere at La Scala in 1922.

The year 1922 also witnessed a new production of Verdi's Rigoletto (final scene below) that featured the soprano Toti Dal Monte, seen at bottom left in costume for her role in Lucia di Lammermoor, another Toscanini enterprise. Bottom right, Rosetta Pampanini, stalwart of the roster, whose specialty was verismo repertory, notably Puccini.

Toscanini's mother, Paolina (left), who died in 1924 at the age of eighty-four, lived to see the rise of Fascism in Italy. At right, the medal awarded Toscanini for leading a concert in the city of Fiume, "liberated" for Italy in 1919 by poet-adventurer Gabriele d'Annunzio (below), who had urged Italy to join World War I and lost an eye as a fighter pilot.

A colorful figure in Italian history, d'Annunzio was an ardent nationalist but an impractical romantic in political matters. The black shirts for his followers in the Fiume occupation influenced Mussolini, as did his swashbuckling personal style and lofty rhetoric, even his handwriting (compare with Duce's on facing page). In failing health, he lived until 1938.

Once again, family troubles weighed on Toscanini: in July 1924 his mother died. Meanwhile, ominous clouds were gathering over Italy. In the wake of postwar unemployment and social instability, a former journalist named Benito Mussolini would step into the breach—starting as a socialist, opposed to the monarchy and the clergy, echoing the tradition Toscanini had learned from his father. In 1919, in the interests of mustering a minority protest vote, Toscanini even was persuaded to run for deputy on the same ticket with Mussolini in Milan, supporting the syndicalist platform of a coalition group called the Sansepolcri̇ti.

By the time Mussolini went national and took the name Fascist Party in 1921, his politics had changed radically. Seeing that socialism had no chance in the postwar climate of fear of Bolshevism (the Russian Revolution was fresh in everyone's mind), in 1920 he aligned himself with the industrialists to help break the power of the striking labor unions. By the time of the Fascist March on Rome in October 1922, when Victor Emmanuel III decided to invite him to form a cabinet and take over the government, he was ready to make accommodations with the Church and the monarchy. Relations between Toscanini and Mussolini chilled in proportion to the latter's interest in personal power. The suicide in December 1923 of Giuseppe Gallignani, ousted by the Fascists as head of the Milan Conservatory, and the murder in June 1924 of the Socialist Party secretary, Giacomo Matteotti, who had dared stand up to Mussolini, were signposts on the road to repression. Democratic processes soon were suspended in Italy.

Though willing to introduce a performance with a national anthem on an appropriate occasion, Toscanini did not consider the Fascist government legitimate or its song "Giovinezza" a national anthem, and he refused to play it. He also refused to allow portraits of Mussolini and the king to be hung in La Scala. After a series of incidents in which the issue of "Giovinezza" was pushed on him, the Maestro was summoned to the police prefecture in Milan, where he stared silently at a spot on the wall while Mussolini lectured him on his uncooperative attitude. It was just the beginning.

A low point in Mussolini's fortunes was his arrest as a radical in 1919 (left); a high point was his March on Rome (second left), resulting in his taking over the government, in 1922. The following year, expanding toward dictatorship, he hoped to conciliate Toscanini and visited La Scala (lower left), posing with the conductor and Toti Dal Monte (in white).

Words of admiration laced the Duce's handwritten message to the Maestro (below). While he posed as a friend of the arts, fiddling (bottom right), the brutality behind the façade became evident with such incidents as the assassination of Socialist Party secretary Matteotti (bottom left), who had dared to denounce the Duce's excesses.

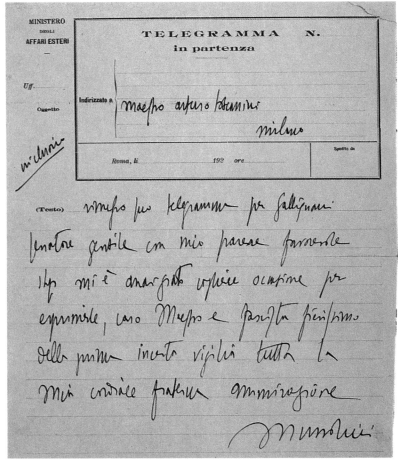

Arrigo Boito (below), poet and composer, for many years advisor to the Teatro alla Scala, died in 1918, leaving unfinished his second opera, Nerone. Fascinating as a literary work, it combined too many historic and symbolic elements to be viable onstage. Moved by loyalty, Toscanini worked on it with fellow conductor Vincenzo Tommasini.

Nerone posed problems, especially its orchestration, an area in which Boito never felt comfortable. When the opera was produced at La Scala in 1924, no expense or effort was spared. The title role was given to Aureliano Pertile (in costume below), a leading tenor of the Toscanini era at the Milan theater, known as an actor and interpreter as well as a singer.

Arrigo Boito, librettist of Verdi's last two operas and composer of *Mefistofele*, had been a great friend to the young Arturo Toscanini, bringing him first into direct contact with Verdi, then to La Scala as its artistic chief. When Boito died in 1918, the completion of his *Nerone* became the responsibility of Toscanini, who shared with Vincenzo Tommasini, another conductor, the task of sorting out the manuscript and orchestrating it. The production at La Scala on May 1, 1924, was one of the most complicated and challenging of Toscanini's career.

Not long after *Nerone* was brought to life, the Maestro learned of the death of another composer friend, Giacomo Puccini, at a clinic in Brussels. At odds during the war years, the two had reconciled, and Puccini was writing a new opera, *Turandot*, for La Scala. Visiting him not long before, Toscanini had been sobered by Puccini's tired appearance and unnatural voice: the composer suffered from cancer of the throat. The final scene of *Turandot*, which had been causing Puccini trouble, lay in the form of a few sketches. These were worked into a performing version by Franco Alfano, but Puccini had asked Toscanini to perform *Turandot* incomplete. That was how he did it at the premiere on April 25, 1926, turning to the audience and announcing in his hoarse voice, "The opera ends here, because at this point the Maestro died."

Mussolini was in Milan but did not attend *Turandot* because of Toscanini's continuing refusal to play the Fascist song "Giovinezza." The firing of anti-Fascists had become commonplace, and there had been pressure on La Scala to get rid of this troublemaker. The contretemps offered hope to the directors of the New York Philharmonic, which Toscanini had started to conduct early in 1926: perhaps now he would become more available. But for two more seasons, 1927-29, the relationship with La Scala continued, Toscanini meanwhile returning to the Philharmonic for midwinter concerts. Now past sixty and bothered by bursitis in his right shoulder and arm, he was beginning to think his days as a theater man should end. As a farewell gesture he took La Scala's *Falstaff* to Vienna and Berlin in the spring of 1929, then agreed to become principal conductor of the Philharmonic, starting in 1930.

When Giacomo Puccini (below, a late photo) died in 1924, Toscanini fell heir to another unfinished opera, Turandot, a fanciful Chinese fairy tale. Another composer, Franco Alfano, wrote the final scene from Puccini's sketches, while publisher Ricordi prepared an ornate edition (left). Sketches at middle and lower left show designs for La Scala premiere.

It was on this staircase in the "violet city" of Peking, before the imperial palace, that Rosa Raisa as Princess Turandot posed her three life-or-death riddles to Spanish tenor Miguel Fleta as Prince Caläf, her audacious suitor. Toscanini was soon to leave La Scala, but first he led a company tour to Vienna and Berlin, depicted by a caricaturist (bottom).

Below, Toscanini with the New York Philharmonic onstage at Carnegie Hall. His decade (1926-36) as guest, then principal conductor, scored a high-water mark for the orchestra, which reached millions via radio, records and tour concerts. His farewell was a benefit program for the orchestra, the hall and the Musicians Emergency Fund on April 29, 1936.

That final concert, with Jascha Heifetz as violin soloist, sold out as soon as it was announced. Early on the morning of the day, though only 140 standing-room passes remained, some 5,000 people started to line up on the street (bottom) in hopes of getting in. Police had trouble restraining the crowd, some of whom broke through an emergency exit.

That Toscanini never meant to turn his back on Europe is clear from the tour on which he led the New York Philharmonic in the spring of 1930, starting at the Paris Opera and including four Italian cities. The tour continued to four German cities as well as Vienna, Brussels, Budapest, Prague and London. Then Toscanini went to the Bayreuth Festival, the Wagner shrine in Bavaria, to lead *Tristan und Isolde* and *Tannhäuser*. Thanks to his admirer Siegfried Wagner, he became the first foreigner to conduct there. Out of reverence for Wagner he refused any salary but took exception to the quality of the orchestra, insisting that some players be replaced. When Siegfried asked, "But Arturo, do you really think they're so bad?" he replied, "No, they're not bad—they're *terrible*!"

In Bologna in May 1931 for concerts commemorating the composer-conductor Giuseppe Martucci, Toscanini entered an ominous new phase of his relationship with the Fascists. Having refused as usual to conduct "Giovinezza," he was set upon and roughed up by a band of thugs as he stepped from his car for the first concert. He escaped to his hotel, which was soon besieged by milling crowds of Fascists. The composer Ottorino Respighi, who had rushed to the hotel from the concert hall, acted as intermediary with the local party secretary, who said the family must leave Bologna by six the next morning or he could not guarantee their safety.

May 1931 Bologna concerts (left) never took place: arriving at hall, Toscanini was assaulted by Fascists. Conducting no more in Italy, he appeared in Bayreuth, where sketch (middle left) shows him. Colleagues there were soprano Nanny Larsén-Todsen, tenor Lauritz Melchior (below left). On balcony (right) with family— Wally, Wanda, Carla, Walter.

Toscanini's first Bayreuth season was 1930, at invitation of Wagner's son, Siegfried (with him, middle of page), who died that summer. Widow of Siegfried, English-born Winifred (at table between conductors Wilhelm Furtwängler and Toscanini), turned out to be an enthusiast for Aldolf Hitler, a personal friend she welcomed to Bayreuth (bottom).

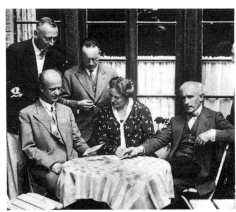

They left for Milan, where their passports were taken and their house was put under surveillance.

Meanwhile, Fascist sympathies seemed to be taking over Bayreuth. Winifred Wagner, widow of the recently deceased Siegfried, was an enthusiastic friend and supporter of Adolf Hitler and had sent him the paper on which to write *Mein Kampf* in prison. Though he led *Parsifal* at the 1931 festival, Toscanini withdrew from *Die Meistersinger* in 1933 after Hitler came to power. His recordings, and those of other protesting musicians, promptly were banned in Germany.

By 1935, the Depression had taken its toll on the New York Philharmonic. Toscanini, weary of the intense work schedule, fearing a decline in artistic standards after ten glorious seasons, decided early in 1936 not to renew his contract.

Tel-Aviv poster announces first season of Palestine Orchestra, inaugurated in December 1936 by Toscanini at urging of violinist friend Bronislaw Huberman, whose hand he shakes (middle left) while acknowledging applause. Program included symphonies by Brahms and Schubert, overtures by Rossini and Weber, Mendelssohn incidental music.

During his sojourn in Israel, Toscanini did extensive sightseeing, visiting with settlers as well as dignitaries, such as statesman Chaim Weizmann (middle right). Below, an earlier photo of music-loving physicist Albert Einstein, long an admirer of the conductor, who wrote to congratulate him for his strong stand against Fascism in Europe.

XXVIII. SALZBURG AND PALESTINE

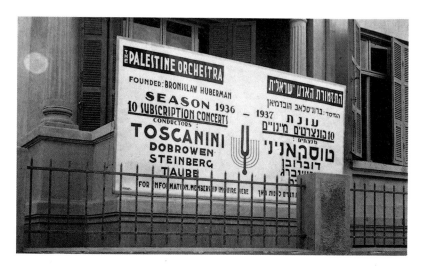

To pay his respects to the German-speaking world of art, Toscanini went to the Salzburg Festival in Austria in the summers of 1934, '35, '36 and '37. There he led the last staged opera performances of his life—Beethoven's *Fidelio,* Verdi's *Falstaff,* Wagner's *Die Meistersinger,* Mozart's *Die Zauberflöte. Die Meistersinger* he had agreed to conduct at Bayreuth in 1933—before refusing Hitler's personal entreaty to return. Toscanini expected other artists to use their influence, too, in protest against Fascism. He argued strenuously with Wilhelm Furtwängler at Salzburg in 1937 for continuing to conduct at Bayreuth. German musicians who chose to stay still clung to the belief they could keep their art above politics. Those who were Jewish, however, had no choice but to leave.

It was in December 1936 that Toscanini visited Palestine, inaugurating and even touring with the newly formed orchestra there. Many members were refugees from European Fascism. Though the purpose of these visits was artistic, they also gave notice of Toscanini's solidarity with the Jewish community, among whom he counted so many friends, relatives and colleagues. The idea of asking Toscanini to lead the Palestine Orchestra had been advanced by the violinist Bronislaw Huberman, who knew the Maestro, and it was enthusiastically seconded by Albert Einstein (himself a violinist of sorts), who wrote from Princeton, "You are not only the unmatchable interpreter of the world's musical literature . . . In the fight against the Fascist criminals, too, you have shown yourself to be a man of greatest dignity." Toscanini and his wife did as much sightseeing as they could between concerts. Prepared by William Steinberg (later conductor of the Pittsburgh Symphony), the orchestra passed muster with Toscanini, who conducted without fee and found himself exhilarated by the visit. He hoped to return and in 1938 was able to do so.

To return to Salzburg in 1938 was, however, an impossibility. The Anschluss of that year, with Hitler's troops marching in to the welcome of a sizable portion of the populace (Hitler was Austrian by birth), closed this door to the famous anti-Fascist. Time was running out for him to deliver his artistic and humanitarian message in Europe.

Left, Toscanini at Neumarkt (near Salzburg) with violinist Adolf Busch, pianist Rudolf Serkin; relaxing at Liefering with his granddaughters and daughter Wanda, then with his wife Carla, daughter Wally, son-in-law Count Emanuele Castelbarco. Mid-left, baritone Mariano Stabile applying makeup as Verdi's Falstaff. Bottom left, conductor Bruno Walter, author Thomas Mann, Toscanini.

As assistant maestro Erich Leinsdorf stands by (below), Toscanini coaches Lotte Lehmann in staging of Fidelio. Below middle, final tableau of Die Zauberflöte with Helge Roswaenge, Jarmila Novotna and, in background at head of stairs, Alexander Kipnis. Bottom: curtain call after Die Meistersinger with Herbert Graf, Lehmann, Hermann Wiedemann, Charles Kullman.

Sketches drawn for the National Broadcasting Company, used in a book about its newly formed NBC Symphony, show two illustrious fellow conductors, Artur Rodzinski (left) and Pierre Monteux, partners in organizing the group before Toscanini's arrival from his summer holiday at the Isolino San Giovanni (below), an island retreat he had rented since 1932.

The Isolino, only a short distance from the town of Pallanza on shore, is the smallest of five islands in Lake Maggiore owned by the Borromeo family. There the Maestro enjoyed his family circle—at bottom right, son Walter, visitor Princess von Wrede, grandson Walfredo, the child's uncle Antonio Fornaroli. Bottom left, program of first NBC broadcast.

XXIX. FAREWELL TO EUROPE

Back in Italy after his last Salzburg performances in the summer of 1937, Toscanini received a visit from Samuel Chotzinoff, emissary from David Sarnoff, chairman of the Radio Corporation of America (RCA) in New York. Sarnoff proposed to organize a radio orchestra especially for Toscanini. Though skeptical about starting a new career at seventy, the Maestro accepted, liking the idea of reaching a large radio public. To organize the orchestra he chose Artur Rodzinski, a respected colleague who also had been a good friend of the family at Salzburg. While Toscanini continued guest conducting in Europe, in the last outposts of Holland and Sweden, Rodzinski auditioned players for the NBC Symphony. When it had been formed, Pierre Monteux and Rodzinski led the first five trial concerts, which were not broadcast. Arriving in New York to hear the last of these, Toscanini praised Rodzinski warmly and started rehearsals the next day. He wasted no time on formalities but walked briskly to the podium, called out "Brahms!" and gave the downbeat. On Christmas night 1937 the first Toscanini-NBC concert went over the air from the newly created Studio 8-H in Radio City, where an invited audience held programs printed on silk to avoid making noise (later, cork and blotting paper were used). Nine more broadcasts followed, plus recording sessions. Having reached the largest audience of his life, Toscanini returned to Italy.

Through telephone wiretaps, Mussolini knew of Toscanini's opinions on such subjects as the Fascists' anti-Semitic policy, which he termed "roba da medio evo" (medieval stuff). Nevertheless, it was not until after the Maestro conducted the BBC Symphony in London in June, then at the first Lucerne Festival in August, that his passport was revoked again—this time because the Duce was annoyed that so many prominent Italians had gone to Switzerland to hear the Lucerne concerts. It took criticism in the world press and intervention by Joseph P. Kennedy, the U.S. ambassador to London with connections at the Vatican, to get Toscanini out of Italy in the fall of 1938. He was not to return for seven and a half years. Had Toscanini not left Italy when he did, he almost certainly would have ended in a concentration camp.

Toscanini's last European concerts before the war took place at the Lucerne Festival, summers 1938-39, where other conductors included Ernest Ansermet (below). In 1939 Toscanini led chamber orchestra in Siegfried Idyll at Triebschen (left), Wagner's villa, then concluded at Kunsthaus with son-in-law Horowitz in Brahms' Concerto No. 2 (middle left).

Meanwhile, back in the U.S.A., Toscanini was leading NBC Symphony (middle below). Returning to Italy in summer 1938, he barely got out with help of Ambassador Kennedy (bottom left). Mussolini (bottom center) was striking militaristic postures at urging of Hitler, seen (bottom right) arriving in Austria for Anschluss.

NBC Symphony toured South America in 1940, visiting Rio de Janeiro, site of Toscanini's unexpected debut fifty-four years earlier. In photo on shipboard, violinist Edwin Bachmann (far left), other musicians. Trip took in São Paulo and two neighboring centers—Montevideo (Uruguay), Buenos Aires (Argentina)—where Toscanini had led opera seasons.

Bottom left, cover of a concert program from Rio during 1940 tour. Right, the Maestro is greeted by Brazilian soprano Bidù Sayão, who had made her U.S. concert debut with him in April 1936 during Philharmonic season at Carnegie Hall in Debussy's La Damoiselle Élue. *Sayão's mother was in audience in 1886 when Toscanini led his first* Aida *in Rio.*

XXX. SYMBOL OF A FREE ITALY

In New York toward the end of 1939 to resume his NBC Symphony broadcasts, Toscanini—though he was not a joiner of organizations—joined the Mazzini Society, made up largely of socialists and liberals who longed for an Italian republic. There was always the hope that Mussolini could be overthrown. It was not until June 1940 that Italy attacked France and President Roosevelt told the American radio public, "The hand that held the dagger has struck it into the back of its neighbor." On board the S.S. *Brazil* for a South American tour with the NBC Symphony, Toscanini locked himself in his stateroom in grief, frustration and fury.

He plainly liked working with the NBC Symphony, however, and his concerts seemed to be giving him a new lease on life. Occasionally he stepped away for guest engagements and benefits with the Philadelphia Orchestra, the New York Philharmonic and the Los Angeles Symphony of his friend Alfred Wallenstein. On July 25, 1943, during a Verdi concert with the NBC, news came that Mussolini had been deposed by his own Grand Council and the government turned over to the king and Marshal Pietro Badoglio. Though the war was far from over, Italian patriots in America took heart, and on September 13 an article appeared in *Life* magazine, signed by Toscanini, urging the Allies not to negotiate a peace with the king and Badoglio but to insist on an Italian republic with a democratic government. Allied peace dealings with Italy split the Mazzini Society, with Toscanini defecting and answering uncompromisingly those who supported the monarchy or favored a pragmatic adjustment.

Toscanini, who had never made a film, did so the month the *Life* article appeared. For the Office of War Information he filmed Verdi's *Hymn of the Nations*, adding the Internationale and "The Star-Spangled Banner" in honor of the Allies. In the *Inno di Mameli*, part of Verdi's original score, he changed the words to read, "Oh Italia, oh patria mia tradita"—"my betrayed country." Scenes of the film were shot in NBC's Studio 8-H and at Wave Hill, the house in Riverdale (northwestern New York City) he rented during 1941-45. After the war he bought nearby Villa Pauline, likewise looking from a hillside over the Hudson River.

For Toscanini's only film, Hymn of the Nations, *cameramen worked in NBC Studio 8-H with the orchestra and at Wave Hill, the Maestro's 1941-45 residence (left), where he was photographed in the living room. Lower left, page of Verdi's* Hymn of the Nations *copied for tenor Jan Peerce by Toscanini, changing words to "My betrayed country."*

For the Red Cross, Toscanini led a "monster concert" on May 25, 1944, with the combined NBC/ Philharmonic orchestras at Madison Square Garden under the banners of the Allies. In September 1943, after Mussolini had been deposed (bottom left, with king and Badoglio), Toscanini had written in Life *magazine (bottom) of his hopes for a postwar Italy.*

TO THE PEOPLE OF AMERICA
by ARTURO TOSCANINI

.... People of America, we are not your enemies and never have been your enemies in the past. We were forced into the role of "enemy" by a vicious and wicked man, Mussolini, who betrayed us for more than 20 years. We never wanted to fight against you, and today we do not want to do it. Only the King of Italy and his bootlicker, Badoglio, both despicable men, are your enemies and want to carry on this war. They are bound by the alliance with Germany, which they endorsed jointly with Mussolini. They cannot be dissociated in any way from the militarist and fascist clique. They cannot be the representatives of the Italian people; they cannot in any way conclude peace with the Allies in the name of Italy, so betrayed by them....

We ask that the Allies permit our volunteers to fight against the hated Nazis under the Italian flag with conditions substantially similar to those of the Free French. Thus alone can we Italians visualize the unconditional surrender of our armed forces without injury to our sense of honor. Give us a chance to fight along with you in your just cause which is also our own cause....

ARTURO TOSCANINI
"Give us a chance to fight along with you in your just cause, which is also our cause"

On August 16, 1943, three weeks after Mussolini was ousted, Allied bombs struck Milan's Teatro alla Scala, below. Hopes for the theater's rebirth were tied to a patriotic desire for the return of Toscanini; posters hailing him were placed outside the battered opera house by Walter Toscanini's brother-in-law Antonio Fornaroli and other anti-Fascists.

Two more years of war, however, remained for Italy. Toscanini contributed toward postwar repair of La Scala but would not go home until a public referendum on the fate of the monarchy was set. Immediately thereafter, he arrived in Chiasso, at the Swiss border, on April 23, 1946. Below, he leaves train with U.S. Army liaison officer Clement Petrillo.

XXXI. RETURN TO ITALY

As soon as the war was over, Toscanini wanted to go back to his homeland, but he refused as long as the House of Savoy remained. Meanwhile, he sent a large sum toward the rebuilding of the Teatro alla Scala, badly damaged by bombs in August 1943. When a public referendum about the monarchy finally was announced, he went home to vote for a republic. It was the spring of 1946.

At the reopening concert of La Scala on May 11, he led a program of Italian composers, inevitably including opera excerpts. One of the soloists was young—the soprano Renata Tebaldi, a recent graduate of the conservatory in Parma that Toscanini had attended. The others—Mafalda Favero, Mariano Stabile, Tancredi Pasero, Giuseppe Nessi—were veterans of prewar seasons with Toscanini at La Scala. On June 2 the Maestro cast his vote in the referendum that abolished the monarchy. After all those years, his father's dream of an Italian republic was realized. And he showed his old fire by canceling visits to Paris and London with the La Scala orchestra after the Allies decided to give the enclave of Tenda and Briga to France: Toscanini opposed any alteration of Italy's boundaries.

As August neared its end, the time approached to return to New York for the 1946-47 NBC season, including a concert performance of Verdi's opera *La Traviata*. In March of that season he passed his eightieth birthday, which he marked by showing interest in the cause of old musicians: he contributed generously to the Musicians' Foundation in New York and the Casa di Riposo, the retirement home founded by Verdi in Milan. Summer brought his fiftieth wedding anniversary, and after another NBC season, which included a concert performance of *Otello*, in the spring of 1948 he stood once more on the podium at La Scala, leading scenes from *Mefistofele* and *Nerone* as a memorial to their composer, Arrigo Boito.

At the end of 1949, Toscanini declined an honorary life senatorship offered by Italian President Luigi Einaudi. "Desiring to end my existence in the same simple state in which I have lived it," he wrote in reply, ". . . I beg you not to interpret my wish as a discourteous or arrogant act, but rather in the spirit of simplicity and humility that inspires it."

On May 11, 1946, little more
than two weeks after his return,
Toscanini reopened La Scala with
a concert of Italian music (poster,
left), warmly greeted by an audience of notables. Symbolizing the
start of Italy's recovery,
this emotional event was drawn
(below) for the cover of Domenica
del Corriere, *Italian Sunday
supplement of Milan's* Corriere
della Sera.

At Isolino, Maestro and wife with
daughter Wally and pianist Ania
Dorfman (rear). Returning from
Italy, he led NBC broadcast of
La Traviata *(middle left) with
Jan Peerce, Licia Albanese, Robert
Merrill, Arthur Newman. In
spring 1949,* Aida *was telecast
(bottom left) with Stich-
Randall, Tucker, Gustavson, Nelli,
Scott, Valdengo (not shown).*

Memorabili serate alla Scala: i concerti diretti da Toscanini

The first and last U.S. musical organizations for which Toscanini worked—the Metropolitan Opera and the NBC Symphony—came together in Dallas on April 30, 1950, when the itineraries of their tours happened to coincide. In station (below), train at left carried the NBC, with Maestro and his grandson, Walfredo, waving to Met conductor Wilfrid Pelletier.

The only leg of the tour on which Toscanini could rest for a few days was the trip from Dallas to Pasadena, which he made by plane while the orchestra proceeded by rail. Thanks to recordings and broadcasts from both the Philharmonic and the NBC years, he was well known to music-lovers, but most were seeing him in person for the first time.

XXXII. A CULMINATING ACHIEVEMENT

Toscanini had fallen into the habit of including a complete opera in most of his NBC Symphony broadcast seasons, and in 1949-50 it was the turn of *Falstaff*, which he had led so often since the work was new. Now there loomed ahead the most extraordinary undertaking of his NBC years, the six-week 1950 tour that would bring the orchestra to twenty American cities. The Maestro was eighty-three, but his enthusiasm was that of a young man. Every ten years, his life had been punctuated by a major tour: the Metropolitan Opera to Paris in 1910, the orchestra of La Scala to the U.S. and Canada in 1920, the New York Philharmonic to Europe in 1930, the NBC Symphony to South America in 1940. In between, there had been shorter tours

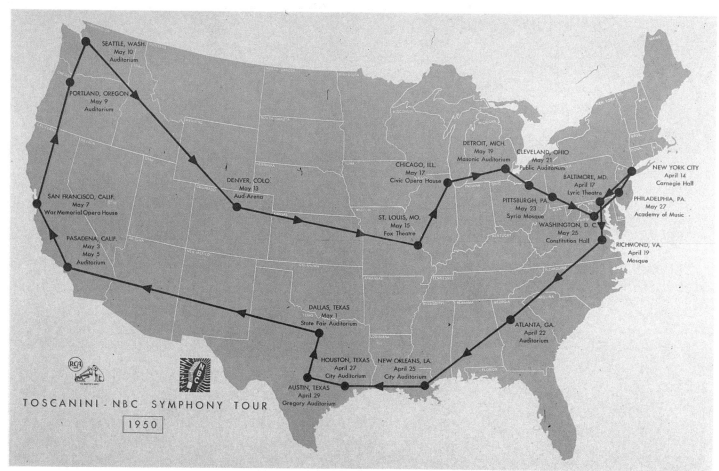

TOSCANINI - NBC SYMPHONY TOUR
1950

When the tour started in New York, son Walter (left) prepared to board with his father while RCA chairman David Sarnoff wished them bon voyage. Not long before, Time magazine had devoted a story to the tireless Maestro, whose cover portrait was the work of Boris Chaliapin, son of Russian bass who had sung with Toscanini at La Scala.

Toscanini visited Williamsburg (top left below), enjoyed sitting on grass in San Francisco (top right) and riding Sun Valley ski lift (lower left). There was even time for fooling: NBC men improvised a "Sad Symphony" (lower right), which he led at picnic. Bottom, 1948 telecast of Brahms Liebeslieder Waltzes: TV gave audiences their first chance to watch Maestro's face rather than just his back.

too—with the Turin orchestra and La Scala. Touring, like the theater, was in Toscanini's blood.

For a month and a half in 1950, a special train became the musicians' home. In every new city, the Maestro would lead the way in sightseeing. He did not want to miss a thing, and his energy left even his twenty-year-old grandson, Walfredo, feeling exhausted. Because the Maestro's wife had been in ill health, she could not come along, but he emerged from the marathon happy and invigorated.

It was to be his last such experience. By that time, the NBC Symphony's home Studio 8-H had been converted for television, and the concerts were being broadcast from Carnegie Hall. Toscanini had suffered a minor stroke in March while exercising on a stationary bicycle as therapy for his knee, which had been bothering him. A heavy blow was the death of his wife, Carla, who succumbed to a heart attack in Milan in mid-June 1951 at seventy-four. Nevertheless, Toscanini was determined to die in harness: "Work I must, otherwise life is unbearable!" he wrote his daughter Wally in October 1951. For the 1951-52 season he led twelve broadcasts, culminating in Beethoven's Ninth Symphony, plus twenty-one recording sessions. In September 1952 he led the orchestra of La Scala for the last time, choosing an all-Wagner program. And in London he undertook a Brahms cycle with the Philharmonia Orchestra. The next NBC season, 1953-54, turned out to be his last. He scheduled *Un Ballo in Maschera*—the first opera he ever attended.

Riverdale-On-Hudson
New York

March 25, 1954

My very dear David:

At this season of the year seventeen years ago you
sent me an invitation to become the Musical Director of an
orchestra to be created especially for me for the purpose of
broadcasting symphonic music throughout the United States.

You will remember how reluctant I was to accept
your invitation because I felt at that time that I was too
old to start a new venture. However, you persuaded me and
all of my doubts were dispelled as soon as I began rehearsing
for the first broadcast of Christmas night in 1937 with the
group of fine musicians whom you had chosen.

Year after year it has been a joy for me to know
that the music played by the NBC Symphony Orchestra has been
acclaimed by the vast radio audiences all over the United
States and abroad.

And now the sad time has come when I must reluctantly
lay aside my baton and say goodbye to my orchestra, and in
leaving I want you to know that I shall carry with me rich
memories of these years of music making and heartfelt gratitude
to you and the National Broadcasting Company for having made
them possible.

I know that I can rely on you to express to everyone
at the National Broadcasting Company who has worked with me
all these years my cordial and sincere thanks.

Your friend,

Arturo Toscanini

Brig. General David Sarnoff
Chairman of the Board
RADIO CORPORATION OF AMERICA
30 Rockefeller Plaza
New York 20, New York

RADIO CORPORATION OF AMERICA
RCA BUILDING
30 ROCKEFELLER PLAZA
NEW YORK 20, N.Y.

DAVID SARNOFF
CHAIRMAN OF THE BOARD

March 29, 1954

Maestro Arturo Toscanini
Riverdale-on-Hudson
New York, New York

Dear Maestro:

Your letter, significantly written on your Birthday,
touched me deeply. I realize that after more than sixty-five
years of absolute dedication to the art of music you have fully
earned the right to lay down your baton. Yet I am saddened, along
with millions of people in America, indeed all over the civilized
world, at the thought that we shall no longer be privileged to look
forward to your broadcasts and concerts which for so many years
ennobled our lives. That you have made your decision at a time
that finds you at the very height of your artistic powers only adds
poignancy to our deprivation....

During these seventeen years of our intimate and happy
association, I have learned from you much that is as vital in
industry as it is in music. Your attitude towards your art and
especially that human instrument - the orchestra - which realized
your musical ideals, became an inspiration to me from the very
first time I watched you at work. You proved so convincingly that
in striving to attain perfection, the leader who seeks to obtain the
maximum from those he leads, must demand the utmost not only
from them but also from himself.

I know, dear Maestro, you will carry with you the love
and gratitude of your many friends and the great multitude, unknown
to you, whose lives you have enriched.

May God bless you and keep you.

Your friend,

David Sarnoff

XXXIII. THE LAST CONCERT

As the 1953-54 NBC Symphony season drew to a close, Toscanini was deeply upset. He knew his conducting days were numbered. During preparations for *Un Ballo in Maschera* the winter before, there were times when he had trouble remembering the music, and other days when he remembered the music but not the words—he of the legendary photographic memory. He sensed pressure within NBC to terminate the orchestra. The concerts were becoming too expensive, though chairman Sarnoff would not stop them as long as Toscanini could still conduct. The Maestro feared his orchestra would be disbanded, leaving the players without jobs.

Toscanini always hated his birthday, for him a reminder of aging and mortality. There was deliberate irony in the fact that he signed his letter of resignation on March 25, 1954, his eighty-seventh birthday. On April 3 he stepped to the podium at Carnegie Hall for the final rehearsal of the Wagner concert that would end the season. In the dawn music of *Götterdämmerung* he corrected what he thought was a wrong entrance by the timpani—but this time, most uncharacteristically, the error was his. Angrily he left the stage without finishing.

At the concert itself on April 4 he conducted—as he would recall afterward—almost as if he were not there. The orchestra sensed his detachment, but no trouble developed until the entrance of the sirens' voices (played by solo strings) in the *Tannhäuser* bacchanal. His protégé Guido Cantelli, in the control booth with program director Don Gillis, saw the Maestro put his hands to his eyes, as if trying to focus his mental image of the score while his baton faltered. Fearing a breakdown of the performance, Cantelli decided the music should be cut off, and for a minute a record of Brahms' First Symphony was substituted. In the hall, the Maestro quickly regained command, and the broadcast went ahead. At the end of the *Tannhäuser*, he had to be reminded that the *Meistersinger* prelude still remained on the program. After leading it in a perfunctory, distracted way, he left and did not return for bows.

At a reception for the NBC Symphony at his home, he never came downstairs. Two musicians found him closeted in his studio. "How can I face my poor orchestra?" he asked them.

As his last years unfolded, Toscanini for some time had been living at Villa Pauline (left top and bottom). There his study (second left) contained bust of Verdi by Vincenzo Gemito, other mementos of composers. In summer he still went to Isolino, where circle included (lower left) conductor protégé Guido Cantelli, Pauline Chotzinoff, daughter Wally.

During final NBC broadcast, his legendary memory faltered for a moment; musicians in the orchestra realized it, though audience did not. Below, he tries to focus again on his mental image of the score. In retirement, he listened to records (bottom left) at Villa Pauline, in whose basement his son, Walter (right), maintained an extensive sound archive.

Soprano Rose Bampton and her husband, conductor Wilfrid Pelletier, were among visitors at Villa Pauline. Below, she listens with Toscanini to test pressing of NBC's final scene from Act I of Wagner's Die Walküre. *Though he approved some further discs for release, Toscanini's exacting standards kept him from viewing his recordings uncritically.*

Involved once more in music-making, he coaches violinist Daniel Guilet (right, bottom picture) in a phrase from a Beethoven string quartet. Guilet, Bernard Robbins (center), violist Emanuel Vardi (behind Toscanini) and cellist Benar Heifetz (not shown) were former NBC players who visited Villa Pauline to offer chamber music. At left, Pelletier.

XXXIV. "NO LONGER A MAESTRO"

In June 1954, two months after his final NBC Symphony concert, Arturo Toscanini led some recording sessions, and the musicians found him his old self: *Aida*, the first music he ever conducted professionally, was also the last. Returning to Milan, he was saddened in August by news of the death of his daughter-in-law, Cia, and the idea of inaugurating the new Piccola Scala with *Falstaff* had to be abandoned after he suffered a mild heart attack. Luchino Visconti, with whom he discussed *Falstaff*, was staging Spontini's *La Vestale* at La Scala, and the Maestro attended rehearsals. In February 1955, with work waiting in New York, he left to "finish in exile." For two more years he reviewed his unpublished recordings, deciding which could be issued. Time weighed heavily, and when the conductor Milton Katims (a former NBC violist) came to visit, Toscanini said, "No, don't call me Maestro—I'm no longer a Maestro."

Despite his usual dislike of his birthday, he was willing to acknowledge his ninetieth, which would have fallen on March 25, 1957. The morning after the family's New Year's Eve party, at which he was in excellent spirits, he suffered a stroke, a cerebral thrombosis. After lingering two weeks in his stricken state, he died the morning of January 16. The funeral at St. Patrick's Cathedral in New York drew a throng, followed by a citywide observance of burial ceremonies in Milan, where forces from La Scala offered the "Libera me" from Verdi's Requiem and—recalling Toscanini's own performance at Verdi's funeral—"Va, pensiero" from *Nabucco*.

The Maestro's son Walter stayed in Villa Pauline a decade longer, carrying on the collection and preservation of his broadcast and rehearsal tapes. After Walter himself suffered a stroke, the house was sold to school developers, who abruptly razed it in December 1980. A microfilm collection of musical manuscripts at the Lincoln Center branch of the New York Public Library, named the Toscanini Memorial Archive, was inaugurated in late 1965. And in late 1986, Toscanini's family donated its tape and document collection to the Library. There also are collections of his performances available for public audition at Wave Hill and at the Museum of Broadcasting in New York City.

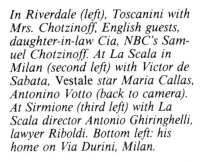

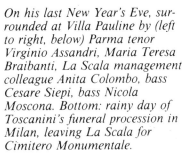

In Riverdale (left), Toscanini with Mrs. Chotzinoff, English guests, daughter-in-law Cia, NBC's Samuel Chotzinoff. At La Scala in Milan (second left) with Victor de Sabata, Vestale star Maria Callas, Antonino Votto (back to camera). At Sirmione (third left) with La Scala director Antonio Ghiringhelli, lawyer Riboldi. Bottom left: his home on Via Durini, Milan.

On his last New Year's Eve, surrounded at Villa Pauline by (left to right, below) Parma tenor Virginio Assandri, Maria Teresa Braibanti, La Scala management colleague Anita Colombo, bass Cesare Siepi, bass Nicola Moscona. Bottom: rainy day of Toscanini's funeral procession in Milan, leaving La Scala for Cimitero Monumentale.

Toscanini's birth house, bought and restored by City of Parma, re-opened in 1987 after earthquake damage. Its simple façade (left) guards memorabilia donated by family, such as painting of Maestro's wife (right). Bottom left: at La Scala Museum, grand-daughter Emanuela Castelbarco with her mother, Wally, and son, Pierfilippo d'Aquarone.

At Conservatory in Parma (middle), in recreation of Toscanini's Milan studio, Vittorio Vaccaro holds book published by Banca Del Monte, written by Gaspare Nello Vetro (left), flanking grandson Walfredo, his cousin Roberto Castellano. In school court-yard, bust by sculptor Corvi. Bottom right: Milan's Piccola Scala, renamed for Toscanini in 1982.

XXXV. THE LEGACY OF TOSCANINI

"Blessed are the arts that don't need interpreters," wrote Arrigo Boito, often quoted by Toscanini. Music, which is no such art, was fortunate to find an interpreter as conscientious as Arturo Toscanini. No single trait explains his eminence. He was possessed of a mania for work, an extraordinary visual memory, leadership charisma and a strong, energetic constitution. These may be the sine qua non of a great career, but they cannot guarantee it. Even more critical was Toscanini's character: nurtured in hardship, he knew the importance of fighting for one's beliefs. Like anyone with high standards, he was doomed to frequent disappointment. "Music—such a beautiful art, such a terrible profession!" he would exclaim, summing up the duality of the everyday world. Because reality is imperfect, a transcendent ideal is the more to be prized—not admired in the abstract, but worked and sweat for.

History draws shifting perspectives, and many who never saw or heard Toscanini in person have sprung up to claim he conducted like a metronome, that his tempos were too fast, that he imposed his concepts rigidly, with a discipline alien to spontaneous music-making. Fortunately, recordings (including rehearsals and broadcasts) remain to make possible a more balanced evaluation. The Toscanini that emerges is remarkably human, constantly exploring and rethinking the works he loved.

From Verdi and his own father, Toscanini picked up the flame of the unity of Italy and carried it high through the years of Fascism and war until his death. As a citizen of the world, Toscanini proved it is possible to stand firm—in his adamant opposition to Mussolini and Hitler, in his insistence on reforming the way opera houses and symphony orchestras were managed. His performances were a commitment to the realization of a composer's vision in a dramatic way: there was always blood in them. A revolutionary in his youth, he championed new music and restructured the musicians' world to make this "terrible profession" more professional. In the words of another Italian maestro, Carlo Maria Giulini, "Toscanini fought terrible battles to achieve things everyone takes for granted today. Even musicians who disagree with him are the direct beneficiaries of his work, his struggle."

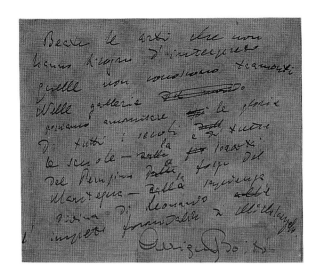

Boito manuscript (left), owned by Toscanini, hails those arts that need no interpreters. Below it, Wave Hill, today an arboretum, also houses its own Toscanini Collection. Spreading his art far and wide, technology has added Compact Discs and videotapes (from NBC telecasts) to the large body of Toscanini interpretations long available on records and cassettes.

Toscanini's archives were kept by his son, Walter, in Riverdale Project at Villa Pauline (below, with engineer John Corbett). Now the family's legacy of word, sound and picture is housed permanently in Lincoln Center branch of New York Public Library (middle). Another treasury of radio and TV performances is Museum of Broadcasting (bottom), New York.

Robert Haas

Arturo Toscanini was the most famous orchestra conductor in history and a world figure, not only for his accomplishments in opera and symphony but for his much publicized opposition to Fascism in Italy and Germany.

A generation of prominent Italian conductors had preceded Toscanini, but none had been able to make fundamental changes in the way theaters and orchestras were organized and run. Toscanini's early reputation was built equally on his phenomenal photographic memory for musical scores and on his uncompromising reforms in the musical establishment. Exacting to work with, he favored an interpretation based on personal commitment to the composer's wishes.

Toscanini saw through the bravado of Mussolini long before many others did. In exile in the U.S. during World War II, he lived to return to a liberated Italy and see an Italian republic become reality. Through broadcasts, records and telecasts, Toscanini's name became a synonym for lofty ideals in classical music as well. His unusually long career was interwoven with many of the foremost personalities and events of musical and political life up through the first half of the twentieth century.

1867 - Arturo Toscanini born March 25, first of four children —and only son—of Claudio, tailor, and former Paola (Paolina) Montani, seamstress, at Borgo San Giacomo 13 in Oltretorrente, working-class section of Parma in northern Italy.
1871 - At age four, taken to see his first opera, *Un Ballo in Maschera.*
1876 - Accepted as day student (later boarding) by Royal School of Music in Parma.
1885 - After nine years' intensive schooling, graduates with highest honors in cello and composition. Engaged by traveling opera troupe as first cellist, an honor for an eighteen-year-old.
1886 - Unscheduled debut as conductor of *Aida* with touring company in Rio de Janeiro, Brazil, June 30. In November, professional debut in Italy as conductor of Catalani's *Edmea* at Teatro Carignano, Turin.
1887 - Plays as second cellist in world premiere of Verdi's *Otello* at Teatro alla Scala, Milan, February 5. Begins decade of conducting in provincial theaters.
1892 - Conducts world premiere of Leoncavallo's *Pagliacci* at Teatro Dal Verme, Milan, and leads Franchetti's *Cristoforo Colombo* at Teatro Carlo Felice in Genoa—only time Verdi hears him conduct.
1893 - Death of his composer friend Alfredo Catalani in Milan, August 7.
1895 - Appointed to form and lead new orchestra in Turin, where he introduces Wagner's *Götterdämmerung* to Italy.
1896 - Conducts world premiere of Puccini'a *La Bohème*, Turin, February 1. Leads first symphony concert, Turin, March 20.
1897 - Marries Carla De Martini, June 21.
1898 - Birth of first child, son Walter, in Turin, March 21. Leads Italian premiere of three of Verdi's *Four Sacred Pieces.* Named artistic director of La Scala at thirty-one and opens Milan season with *Die Meistersinger*, December 26.
1900 - Leads world premiere of Leoncavallo's *Zazà* at Teatro Lirico, Milan; romantic involvement with leading lady, Rosina Storchio. Birth of first daughter, Wally, January 16.
1901 - Conducts at Verdi's funeral in Milan. Second son,

Giorgio, born September 28.
1903 - Quits La Scala in April after disagreements with audience, new board of directors.
1906 - Death of father Claudio and son Giorgio. Return to La Scala and controversy with Richard Strauss over Italian premiere of the composer's opera *Salome.*
1907 - New orchestra pit at La Scala, built at Toscanini's insistence, inaugurated with *Götterdämmerung.* Birth of second daughter, Wanda, December 5.
1908 - After further disagreements at La Scala, leaves with manager Gatti-Casazza to run Metropolitan Opera, New York. Debut there in November 16 *Aida* with Caruso.
1910 - Leads world premiere of Puccini's *La Fanciulla del West* at Metropolitan, December 10.
1913 - U.S. debut as symphony conductor, at Met. First U.S. performance of *Boris Godunov*, March 13. Commemoration of Verdi birth centennial, Busseto.
1915 - Resigns from Met after series of disillusionments and disagreements. Returns to Italy as World War I begins.
1917 - Leads military band for soldiers at front; decorated for bravery under fire.
1918 - Death of composer-librettist friend Arrigo Boito in Milan, June 10.
1919 - Runs for parliamentary deputy on ticket of Sansepolcristi, socialist splinter group headed by former journalist Benito Mussolini.
1920 - Named "plenipotentiary director" of La Scala; theater becomes a public corporation. Toscanini forms new La Scala orchestra and takes it on North American tour, also making first records for Victor in Camden, New Jersey.
1921 - La Scala reopening.
1922 - Mussolini seizes power after March on Rome. Beginning of Toscanini's antagonism toward new dictator.
1924 - Leads world premiere of Boito's *Nerone* at La Scala. Death of mother and Puccini. Socialist Party Secretary Matteotti assassinated by Fascists.
1926 - Conducts New York Philharmonic for first time. World premiere of Puccini's *Turandot* at La Scala.
1927 - Leads his first radio broadcast, with N.Y. Philhar-

monic. Named the orchestra's regular conductor.
1929 - La Scala tour to Vienna and Berlin. Named principal conductor of N.Y. Philharmonic. Birth of first grandchild, Walfredo, August 16 in Milan.
1930 - Philharmonic tour of Europe. Toscanini first foreigner to conduct at Wagner's Bayreuth Festival.
1931 - Attacked by Fascist thugs in Bologna for refusing to play party anthem "Giovinezza." Will not conduct in Italy as long as Mussolini remains.
1933 - Refuses to return to Bayreuth after Hitler takes power in Germany. Granddaughter Emanuela Castelbarco born to daughter Wanda, June 19.
1934 - Birth of second granddaughter, Sonia Horowitz, to daughter Wanda, October 2.
1935 - Debut at Salzburg Festival, non-Fascist musical center, conducting last staged operas of his career.
1936 - Retires from N.Y. Philharmonic. First trip to Palestine to inaugurate Symphony.
1937 - Begins NBC Symphony broadcasts, December 25.
1938 - Conducts orchestra of refugees from Fascism at Lucerne, Switzerland. Returns to Palestine for more concerts.
1939 - Last concert in Europe until after World War II, in Lucerne with son-in-law Vladimir Horowitz as piano soloist.
1940 - South American tour with NBC Symphony. Italy attacks France and enters World War II.
1943 - Fall of Mussolini government. Toscanini films *Hymn of the Nations.*
1944 - Red Cross benefit concert, Madison Square Garden.
1946 - Returning to Italy, Toscanini reopens rebuilt La Scala with concert, votes in election for Italian republic.
1947 - 50th wedding anniversary.
1948 - First telecast, with NBC Symphony, March 20.
1950 - NBC Symphony U.S. tour.
1951 - Death of wife, June 23, age nearly seventy-four.
1954 - Last concert with NBC. Retires from 68-year career.
1955 - Returns to U.S. to work with son Walter on recordings.
1957 - Dies January 16 at Riverdale home after stroke suffered on New Year's Eve. Burial in Milan.

ACKNOWLEDGMENTS

The authors are grateful for the help and advice of Harvey Sachs, author of *Toscanini* (Lippincott 1978). For further assistance in locating pictures and verifying information they are indebted to Lillina Monti Arenosto, Milan; Rose Bampton, New York; Francesco Castellano, Milan; Victor Civita, Rio de Janeiro; Carlo Clausetti, Casa Ricordi, Milan; Felicity Dell'Aquila, New Rochelle; Arthur De Santis, Elite Publishing, New York; Antonio José Faro, Teatro Municipal, Rio de Janeiro; Gilberto Ferrez, Rio de Janeiro; Gerald Fitzgerald, *Opera News*, New York; José Fornaroli, Buenos Aires; Mortimer Frank, curator, Toscanini Collection at Wave Hill, New York; Josephine Inzerillo, Italian State Tourist Office (E.N.I.T.), New York; Carlos Martinez-Saravia, director, Museo del Teatro Colón, Buenos Aires; Anna Naldi and Eliane Perez, Biblioteca Nacional, Rio de Janeiro; Hector Pantalone, Buenos Aires; Mrs. Jan Peerce, New York; Olga Schmid, Zurich; Allan Steckler, New York; Giampiero Tintori, Museo Teatrale alla Scala, Milan; Vivian Treves, Elite Publishing, New York; Robert A. Tuggle, Metropolitan Opera Archives, New York; Gaspare Nello Vetro, author of *Il Giovane Toscanini*, and Vittorio Vaccaro of Banca Del Monte, Parma, publishers of that book. The authors wish to thank the publisher, Peter G. Treves, for his vision in initiating this project and his patience in seeing it to completion; also Rhonda Holman, Elaine Kones and Elaine Toscanini for invaluable help in proofreading. They wish to express special appreciation to the late Walter Toscanini, whose photographs formed the foundation of this book, and whose love for his father, and for historical accuracy, proved a challenging, inspiring example.

ILLUSTRATION CREDITS

(t/m/b = top/middle/bottom; l/c/r = left/center/right)
ABRIL PRESS, SAO PAULO: title page.
ARCHIVIO FOTOGRAFICO DEL TEATRO ALLA SCALA, MILAN: 29 br; 71 2nd l.
ROSE BAMPTON, N.Y.: 70 b.
THE BETTMANN ARCHIVE, N.Y.: 32 bl; 40 t, b; 46 t; 47 bl; 53 br; 61 bl.
BIBLIOTECA NACIONAL, RIO DE JANEIRO: 12 t, b; 13 tr, bl.
CASA MUSEO PUCCINI, TORRE DEL LAGO: 55 tr.
CASSA DI RISPARMIO DELLE PROVINCIE LOMBARDE.
CIVICO ARCHIVIO FOTOGR. CASTELLO SFORZESCO, MILAN 64 ml, bl
CULVER PICTURES, N.Y.: 63 t.
E.N.I.T. (ITALIAN STATE TOURIST OFFICE), N.Y.: 4 tr; 5 tl, ml; 50 bl; 72 br.
JOSÉ FORNAROLI, BUENOS AIRES: 33 bl/r.
FRANKLIN MINT, FRANKLIN CENTER, PA.: 74
JOHN W. FREEMAN, N.Y.: 13 tl.
LIFE MAGAZINE. N.Y.: 63 bc/r.
LA MANDRIA (LUIGI MEDICI DEL VASCELLO), TURIN: 7 tr.
METROPOLITAN OPERA ARCHIVES, N.Y.: 43 ml.
MUSEO DEL TEATRO COLON, BUENOS AIRES: 32 tl, tr, ml; 33 tl.
MUSEO DEL RISORGIMENTO, MILAN: 7 br.
MUSEO TEATRALE ALLA SCALA, MILAN: front cover; 11 bc/r; 14 top 3; 15 bl/r; 19 tl, bl; 20 bl; 21 ml/c, tc/r; 30 bl; 32 br; 34 t, ml; 35 tl, ml, bl; 50 tl/r, b/c; 51 mc/r.
NATIONAL GEOGRAPHIC MAGAZINE, WASHINGTON, D.C.: 43 tr ©1964.
NBC, N.Y.: 31 mr; 60 tl/r; 61 mr; 65 ml, bl; 66 t, b; 67 t, br; 69 tr.
N.Y. PUBLIC LIBRARY THEATER COLLECTION: 73 mr.

N.Y. TIMES: 47 br. Copyright © 1915 by The New York Times Company. Reprinted by permission.
OPERA NEWS MAGAZINE, N.Y.: 15 ml, mc, mr; 17 tr; 19 tr, br; 20 tl/r; 29 tr; 31 tl (Francis Robinson Collection), br; 37 br; 39 tl; 40 ml/r; 41 br; 42 tl/r, b; 43 tl, br; 45 tr, br; 47 tl, mr; 48 tr; 54 b.
MRS. JAN PEERCE, N.Y.: 63 ml.
G. RICORDI & C.—ARCHIVIO FOTOGRAFICO, MILAN: 17 tl, ml, bl; 21 bl; 28 t; 29 tl; 55 tl, ml, bl.
RIZZOLI/DOMENICA DEL CORRIERE, 65 br.
STEPHEN ROZENFELD, NEW ROCHELLE: 51 ml.
HARVEY SACHS, LORO CIUFFENNA: 5 tc, mr; 11 tl/r; 57 tl.
MICHAEL SISCA, LA FOLLIA DI NEW YORK: 20 br; 37 bl, 3rd l; 41 tr, bl; 44 b; 48 tl.
TIME MAGAZINE: 67 bl. Copyright © 1948 by Time Inc. All rights reserved. Reprinted by permission from TIME.
TOSCANINI COLLECTION AT WAVE HILL, N.Y.: 24 b; 25 ml, bl; 62 t, bl/r.
TOSCANINI ARCHIVES (CASA NATALE), PARMA: 44 tl.
COLLECTION WALTER & WALFREDO TOSCANINI, N.Y.: front endpapers; 4 tl; 5 tr; 6 t, b; 7 tl, ml, bl; 8 t; 9 ml; 10 tl, bl; 11 bl; 13 bc; 14 bl; 15 tl/r; 16 tl; 17 br; 18 tl, bl; 21 tl/r; 22 bl/r; 23 tl/r, mr, bl/r; 26 tl/r, b; 27 tl, bl, tr; 28 b; 29 bl; 30 tl; 31 ml, bl; 33 tr, mr; 34 mr, b; 36 tl/r; 37 tl/r, ml, b 2nd l; 38 tl/r; 39 tr, bl/r; 41 tl, ml; 42 m; 45 tl, mr, bl; 48 m; 49 tl/r, bl/r; 51 tl, bc; 52 tl/r, b; 53 tl, 3rd l, tr; 54 t; 55 br; 57 tc/r, mc/r; 59 2nd l/r; 60 bl/r; 61 tl/r, ml, bc; 63 mr; 64 t; 65 tl/r; 67 tc/r, mc/r; 68 t, b; 69 tl, 2nd l, 3rd l, bl/r; 70 l; 71 tl, 3rd l, tr, br; 72 tr; 73 tl, bl, tr.
ROBERT A. TUGGLE, N.Y.: 13 br.
UPI/BETTMANN NEWSPHOTOS, N.Y.: 53 bl; 56 bl; 57 br; 61 br; 63 bl.
GASPARE NELLO VETRO, PARMA: 4 b; 8 b; 9 tl, bl/c/r; 72 tl.
VITA TEATRALE IN LOMBARDIA, ©1982: 16 bl; 21 br; 27 br; 35 tr, br.

PHOTOGRAPHERS

EUGENIO AVANZI, BUENOS AIRES: 33 tr, mr.
MARIO CARRIERI, MILAN: 21 br; 27 br; 35 tr, br.
AIME DUPONT, N.Y.: 40 mr; 42 tl/r; 46 t.
ELLINGER, SALZBURG: 59 tr, br.
GIOVANNI FERRAGUTTI, PARMA: 72 ml.
HERB GEHR, LIFE MAGAZINE ©1943 TIME INC.: 63 br.
ROBERT HAAS, N.Y.: 59 3rd l/c; 75.
SUSANNE WINTERNITZ HOELLER, SALZBURG: 59 tl.
ROBERT HUPKA, N.Y.: back endpapers.
IRENE LOPEZ, MILAN: 38 b; 71 bl.
LIONEL MAPLESON, N.Y.: 43 br.
GRETCHEN McHUGH, N.Y.: 73 ml.

ALBERT MOLDVAY: 43 tr.
STEVEN MARK NEEDHAM, N.Y.: 73 br.
HECTOR PANTALONE, BUENOS AIRES: 33 bl/r.
ERIO PICCAGLIANI, MILAN: 71 2nd l.
EZIO QUIRESI, CREMONA: 16 bl.
ROTHMAIER, SALZBURG: 59 bl.
HARVEY SACHS, LORO CIUFFENNA: 5 tc, b; 9 br; 72 mr.
WALFREDO TOSCANINI, N.Y.: 69 2nd l; 72 tr; 73 bl.
WALTER TOSCANINI, N.Y.: 59 2nd l/c; 67 tc/r, mc/r; 69 tl; 70 t; 71 tl/r.
DAN WEINER, N.Y.: 73 tr.
S. WEISSENSTEIN, TEL-AVIV: 58 t, m.

PAINTERS & GRAPHIC ARTISTS

AUTORI: 55 br.
L. BECHSTEIN: 35 tr, br.
GIOVANNI BOLDINI: 20 tl.
UMBERTO BRUNELLESCHI: 55 ml.
CAGNONI: 27 tl, bl.
CAO: 20 bl; 33 tl.
ENRICO CARUSO: 20 br; 37 bl, 3rd l; 41 tr, bl; 44 b; 48 tl.
BORIS CHALIAPIN: 67 bl.
S. DE ALBERTIS: 7 tr.
A. EDEL: 15 br.

N. D. KUZNETSOV: 36 tl.
ARTURO RIETTI: front cover.
GIAMBATTISTA SANTONI: 51 mr.
HANS SCHLIESSMANN: 40 ml.
BETTINA STEINKE: 60 tl/r.
ANTONIO STROPPA: 29 br.
JAMES JOSEPH JACQUES TISSOT: 13 tl.
DARIO VITERBO: title page.
F. ZENNARO: 7 br.
ZUCCARELLI: 15 bl.